Lawrenc

Champagne Lady
Roberta Linn

THE AUTHOR MURDERS — Eric Meeks

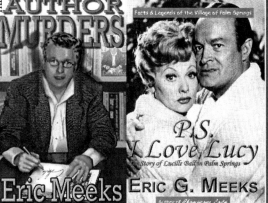

Facts & Legends of the Village of Palm Springs — P.S. I Love Lucy — The Story of Lucille Ball in Palm Springs — ERIC G. MEEKS — Author of Champagne Lady

Lawrence Welk's First Television — Champagne Lady — Roberta Linn — As Told To ERIC G. MEEKS — Author of P.S. I Love Lucy

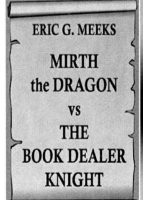

ERIC G. MEEKS — MIRTH the DRAGON vs THE BOOK DEALER KNIGHT

Facts and Legends of the Village of Palm Springs — WITCH of TAHQUITZ — A Morbidly Real Tale of Western Horror — ERIC G. MEEKS — "The Indians won't going to like this."

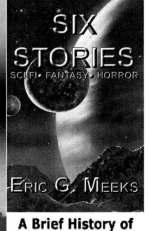

SIX STORIES — SCI-FI · FANTASY · HORROR — ERIC G. MEEKS

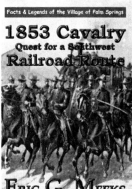

Facts & Legends of the Village of Palm Springs — 1853 Cavalry Quest for a Southwest Railroad Route — ERIC G. MEEKS — Author of WITCH OF TAHQUITZ

SELLING SPACE SHARES — A Short Story — ERIC G. MEEKS

A Brief History of Copyright Law — Eric G. Meeks

Other Works by Eric G. Meeks

Fiction
The Author Murders
Witch of Tahquitz
Six Stories

Non-Fiction
Lawrence Welk's First Television Champagne Lady: Roberta Linn
Not Now Lord, I've Got Too Much to Do
The History of Copyright Law
Reversing Discrimination

99¢ Short Stories
Apollo Thorn: Moons of Jupiter: Corporate Wars
Mirth the Dragon vs the Book Dealer Knight
Vampire Nightmare
Selling Space Share

Edited by Eric G. Meeks
1853 Cavalry Quest for a Southwest Railroad Route

Websites
https://www.facebook.com/eric.g.meeks
http://ezinearticles.com/?expert=Eric_G._Meeks
http://www.flickr.com/photos/ericgmeeks/

Lawrence Welk's First Television

Champagne Lady Roberta Linn

As Told To

Eric G. Meeks

MeeksEric@hotmail.com

Horatio Limburger Oglethorpe, Publisher

I would like to dedicate this book to my mother, my brother Bill, my children Angela and Fred, and to all my fabulous friends and fans who have been there always. Much love…

And to Eric Meeks for helping me put the book together.

Roberta Linn

Foreword

The decision to write this book was really prompted by the need to share an experience that changed my life forever – an experience I was afraid to share or talk about for many years for fear that I would be looked upon as weird or might have had a story that was totally made up.

My out of body experience was in 1958. I was very ill, with pneumonia twice (in both lungs) in six months, given an anti-biotic called Chloromycetin, which seemed to cure the first bout. I had singing engagements in Las Vegas at the Sands hotel and the Moulin Rouge in Hollywood that were very important to my career. So, in spite of being very tired and not strong enough to go back to work, yet being very young, I was back at work singing, dancing and you know doing the whole 'the show must go on' thing which I'd been told all my life. I collapsed in Vegas and was air ambulanced back to Cedars Lebanon hospital in Holly-wood.

I was given the anti-biotics again - a drug so power-ful that when taken in large doses can cause death. My mother didn't know this and I was so ill all she could do was hope and pray that the treatment I was receiving was the best available. Cedars had an impeccable reputation and what was a girl and her mom to do but follow the advice of their doctors?

I had the largest lab bill they had ever seen during my stay there, but I wasn't responding to the treatments. I couldn't eat, eliminate, I started to swell and my skin was red. I must have looked like a turkey that was in the oven too long.

KTLA, the television station where we started the Lawrence Welk show, was saying prayers for me every hour. I wasn't allowed to have the TV on in my room, but one of the nurses accidentally turned it on and I heard that I was dying. The announcer was asking viewers around the country to pray for me. People sent flowers (and prayer cards), so many the halls of the hospital were like a rose garden,

I'd been in the hospital for about three weeks and my mother and Father Michael Montoya, who was the head Padre at San Gabriel Mission, were sleeping on cots in room.

Then it happened.

I was in a tunnel of bright lights, up above, watching the scenario going on around me. My mother kept calling my name, "Roberta, Roberta. Speak to me," and I was answering her but she couldn't hear me. I watched her crying, nurses working over me, doctors being called into the room, and Father Montoya praying and holding my mother. All the while I'm floating up above, a euphoric feeling, no pain, I could see what looked like a figure at the far end of a lighted tunnel passageway though I couldn't see a face just a person. As I looked back at my mother I kept thinking I can't leave her and I kept saying, "Not now Lord, I've got too much to do."

The Lord must have heard my prayers, and gave me back the years I am still enjoying. And what a life it has been. This I would like to share with you.

And oh, by the way, after seeing TV shows and

reading books, about other persons who have had out of body experiences very similar to mine I feel I can share this with you and feel completely comfortable in doing so.

May God bless you and yours always.

Roberta Linn.

Table of Contents

Champagne Lady

HAPPINESS

Happiness is like a beautiful butterfly with many colors
It floats in and out of our lives as a butterfly does
Silently landing on the petals of our lives

Sometimes it lingers for a while
enjoying its relationship with the petal
But there are times when it barely lands before it must fly away
And the petal waits, waits alone
Hoping that the beautiful butterfly will find its way back soon
Oh, make it soon!
Make it Soon!

Roberta Linn

Roberta Linn

The first dress my mother made for me was for a recital
where I sang "My Sweet Little Alice Blue Gown."
I was four years old.

Defying Gravity

"I WAS BORN IN A LITTLE TOWN in Iowa called Gravity," and so began the story of Roberta Linn's life. "If you didn't look quick you'd miss it," she added with a nod of her head.

Daddy was a real good ball player. My mother was a farmer's daughter and my Grandfather was the Mayor of the city next door, which was Bedford. This is down in the Southwest corner of the state, near Omaha.

My mom was Madge Evelyn Bristow and my Daddy's name was Sam Dubin.

I won't tell you my birth year, but I will tell you I was born in the middle of a storm, a blizzard, on April 30. Maybe we'll get to the year later. I was born in a farmhouse and my Grandmother was actually the midwife. Her name was Dora Bristow.

Dad was barnstorming with the Casey Stengel All Stars through Iowa in either 1920 or 1921. Barnstorming was when players in the minor leagues went out and played against the little towns all through the Midwest.

He met my mom; she was at one of the ball games.

My Grandpa was a big baseball fan too. He raised poultry for the Armour meat company. He had a big farm, raised corn and of course poultry too. His name was Albert

3

My Mother, Madge Eve-
lyn Bristow, taken for
her graduation photo
from Bedford High
School, Class of 1920.

My Daddy, Sam Dubin,
while he was still in college back in Westmin-
ster, Missouri. This was
taken shortly before he
playedCfor the Casey
Stengel All-Stars and
met my mother.

Bristow.

My mom and dad fell in love. So they got married and dad stayed there in Gravity. Grandpa declared, "We're not going to have my daughter traveling with any baseball teams." Then Grandpa had dad join the Bedford city baseball team.

My brother Bill had just been born when my dad and my Grandpa had invested in truck loads of Minks and they thought they were going to be able to sell them. They'd bought them out of Canada and then the stock market broke all they got was ten cents on the dollar. They lost everything.

I didn't come along till much later. My Grandpa died before I was born. My Mothers brother and my Dad ran the farm until finally they all decided to go out to California. They'd lost everything back there in Iowa and I was just a little baby when we came out to California. My Mother, my brother (Bill), and myself moved out as a family. Later, my Grandmother came out and eventually my mothers' sister and brother came out. So the whole Bristow family was out here.

We came out on a Union Pacific train. Dad stayed back to sell the business and then drove out in his car, a Whippit. A car like a model A Ford but the company went out of business. The family landed in Huntington Park. My Grandmother and Aunt and Uncle all lived around each other. Mom got an apartment.

Mother got a job as a legal secretary for a lawyer. She was stenographer. She could take shorthand at about 180 words a minute.

GENTS 25c   LADIES FREE

DANCE

AND ENTERTAINMENT

— BY —

ELLA SARKA AND HER
PERSONALITY ORCHESTRA

4433 E. 58TH ST., MAYWOOD

SATURDAY NITE
AUG. 18TH. 8 P. M.

I always kept the business card of my first
real voice instructor, Ella Sarka.

From the movie Senor Jim, a Monogram Film, with Conway Terrill and Barbara edford. I was about 6 years old.

6

Earliest Memories

I remember one time Daddy putting me on a chair in this Italian restaurant, down in San Diego. I still remember it clearly. There was a garden outside with Chianti bottles hanging and the table cloths were checked red and white. I sang 'By the River St. Marie,' a song daddy taught me. All the people came up and told him I should be in show business. That's when I first thought I was going to be an entertainer. Because everybody was saying, "She could be another Shirley Temple."

Dad used to have me call him Mr. Mitchell when he took me places and for auditions, because it wasn't cool to have your father as an agent. So, I used to call him Mr. Mitchell.

I don't know whether that started there in San Diego, but I do remember people rushing up and hugging me and that's my first step into knowing I was going to be doing things.

I had a natural ear. Mom and Dad would sing. Bill would sing. The whole family was musical. Mom read music very well and also played the piano, so, she could teach me my songs.

My earliest memories were singing lessons with Ella Sarka, my first singing teacher, when I was three. I used to

My big brother Bill, at 18 years old when he enlisted
in the U.S. Army Air Corp and became a mechanic.
He served from Oct. 1942 to Feb.1946 and did his
training at Wheeler Fields, Arizona, before being
shipped off to the Pacific

take a little brown bag with my lunch in it and for twenty five cents I got a lesson. She lived till not too long ago. I'd go over to her house and she'd teach me the scales. My brother Bill would take me.

Ella Sarka used to take a lot of her students to all kinds of events; pavilions in parks, weddings, theatres, etc., so we could sing and dance and get used to being in front of an audience.

There was a place called Topsy's where I used to wear a strapless gown my mom made and I'd sit on a piano with a rose and a handkerchief and sing 'My Man.' I was about this big (she raised her hand to about knee high then suppressed a chuckle). This was a mobster's hangout in SouthGate, California. The thing I remember was they had a can that looked like a Kitty Cat which they used to collect money for the band and I'd come out and sing and dance and people would throw money on the floor. Then, my brother Bill would crawl out and scoop it up. That's what we'd eat on that night. I was still only three or four years old. Times were tough and money was short.

Central Castings

In those days, there was an office called Central Castings where everybody in Hollywood registered to do bit parts or extra parts in movies. Daddy signed the whole family up with Central Casting and then the calls began. The Hollywood studios were doing a lot of musicals with children. Bill was doing it, I was doing it, my Mom was doing it, because we could make more money in a day as an extra than a person could earn all week working elsewhere. So, we started doing bit parts in movies.

There's one I remember most that I started in and never knew the name of the movie till recently. I was watching the Ted Turner station and I remember there was this man who had a mule and he was walking up this long ramp like he was going to Heaven and I was playing an angel, a cherub. I was hanging on wires from this sound stage at Warner Brothers and they had little wings on me and a little toga. (She laughed her girlish laugh again at the memory of it). And this man is singing, I'm going to Heaven on a mule. Well, all these years I never knew who that man was. It was Al Jolson and it must have been the last movie he did at Warner Brothers.

I also worked with Ronald Coleman. I played a little crippled girl. I can remember having to walk down this huge

10

stairway with a brace on my leg. It was scary.

I worked with Pat O'Brien, and Shirley Temple, and Ann Sheridan, and Cary Grant, and Clark Gable, and Jimmy Durante, and Anna Mae Wong, and many more really great stars. I was doing all these movies.

You always registered through Central Castings and they called you for the movie auditions and interviews. But there was this short movie I did about the life of Louis Pasteur. It was a short special from the Pete Smith Shorts a production company which shot from the Hal Roach studios. It was funny, I was on the set this day and they had dogs specially trained to jump just past you and they put shaving cream on the dogs faces so they looked like they had rabies. There was a little girl working on the set who they had set up to have this dog jump at her. But, each time the dog would jump this girl would freeze, she couldn't scream. So my mother says, "Go on over there and tell them you can do it," because you can make more money. The role was considered a bit part instead of an extra.

I went over and told the director, I can do it, and he says, OK. They get me set up and the first time the dog jumped I froze too. Nothing would come out and then the second time I made it. I let out a scream that shook the walls. But, it was pretty scary seeing this big dog jump at me with all this stuff on him like he had rabies.

Eventually at Hal Roach studios, I did Babes in Toyland with Laurel and Hardy. I was in the school scenes, with the kids and I did the second series of the "Our Gang" comedies, plus several other movies.

This one day I was on the set with Cary Grant and Jimmy Durante and I had a little paddle with the ball on a rubber band. Cary Grant asked if he could play with it. But, he broke it and he felt so bad he sent someone out and got a dozen of them. He brought them back and I sat there and played paddle boards with Cary Grant and Jimmy Durante on every break. What kid wouldn't have loved that. Even my mom was jealous.

As a child actor you're required to go to school so many hours on the set, every day,which was kind of fun. We had to have so many hours of school including reading, writing and arithmetic, etc. It was required by law and we could only work a limited amount of many hours.

Between movies, I went to Hollywood professional school. That's where all the kids who were doing movies studied. Other than the three R's, you learned singing and dancing and acting and all the things that went along with movies. I went there from my entry age into school. The studios, in most cases, would pay for this while you were working.

I worked with child stars Scotty Beckett and David Holt. I also worked with Dickie Jones, who was the voice of Pinocchio in the original Disney movie. He was my little singing and dancing partner. He and his mom were living on the streets and my mom and dad took them in. They lived with us for a long time. He got really lucky, eventually as a teen, and landed his own western TV series.

I was set to do the part that Jane Withers did with Shirley Temple at Twentieth Century Fox and what happened was, I was smaller and younger than Shirley Temple and her mother would not have me. I'd learned all the dances, all the songs, and everything, but because of my size Shirley's mom put a stop to me. She wanted someone who was bigger and older and I didn't get the part. So, Jane Withers got it instead of me. That was a heartbreak. But, Jane did a great job.

I did other movies with Shirley and was the only one of the kids on the set that Mrs. Temple would let go into

Shirley's dressing room. It was absolutely gorgeous. Everything was to scale for a little girl; the dressers, the mirrors, the couch. It was all pink and white. I'll never forget that dressing room as long as I'll live. I'd never seen a dressing room like that and, wow, it was unbelievable. All the other kids would pull Shirley's hair and scream around her. My mother would never let me do any of those things. I think because of my mother's discretion, Mrs. Temple felt it was OK for me to go in and play. Everything was so beautiful. I have difficulty in telling you how pretty it really was. She was a big star and a very sweet and talented little girl.

In my youthful career, I got to dance with Bill Robinson, who was Mr. Bo Jangles. I was a really good tap dancer. I actually studied with a top teacher who lost the use of his legs and taught me by tapping his cane on the floor. It was a style called intricate tap dancing using heel and toe similar to the Sammy Davis style.

Another time, I did a show one time where I couldn't find the wings while on stage at the Carthay Circle theatre, which was a big theatre, and I crawled out from under the curtain right between the legs of Dick Powell. It was there where all these big movie benefits were held and all the major stars performed. I think even the Oscars were held there years ago.

But I remember it so vividly. It was a huge stage and I was so little. I couldn't make it to the wings of the stage, so I crawled out from under the curtain and between Dick Powell's legs and he started laughing. He picked me up and he couldn't stop laughing. We actually sang together and I tap danced.

I also worked for Mervyn LeRoy in a movie called" Anthony Adverse," filmed at Warner Brothers studios, where I played Olivia DeHaviland's little sister. Mr. LeRoy and I, somehow through fate, our paths crossed again and again many times.

Anthony Adverse is a story about a very wealthy family with an Italian family as servants, the Guiseppe's, who have eight children. The servant father wins the lottery and gains so much money he buys himself and all the children their very own carriages. There was a big scene on the back lot at night out at Warner brothers, where all of us children came around the front of the court house with our carriages. There were hundreds of extras with torches in a big crowd cheering as we rode by. My carriage had a big white horse and, when it was my turn to appear, one of the extras burned my horse's ear with a torch and he reared up in the middle of all of these people, came down on some of them and threw the carriage over.

Mervyn LeRoy, who was directing, of course became frantic, because people were hurt and he saw that I had been thrown out of the carriage. Mervyn came running and picked me up in his arms and carried me, calling my mother on his speaker.

At the time, I worked under the name of Alberta Dugan. But, Mervyn called me the Irish Wop, because I had an Irish name but in the movie I was Maria Giuseppe. He was a great man and a fantastic director and producer.

As I said, Mervyn LeRoy and I seemed to cross paths several times. Years later in Palm Springs, when I was at a party with a very dear friend, named Ray Ryan, who was a very famous man in the early Palm Springs era, I ran into Mervyn. The party was at Raymond Loewy's house, the gentleman who designed the Studebaker, it was a gorgeous home in the plush movie colony area of the desert. There was a piano player playing and Ray asks me if I'll sing his favorite song which was Melancholy Baby. So, he picks me up and puts me on the piano. I sang for Ray, not trying to impress anyone, and I see this man looking at me from across the room. He walked towards me and said, "You look just like Helen Morgan and you sound just like Helen Morgan. I'm doing her life story for Warner Brothers. I want you to call me."

I said, ""Do you remember who I am?" I knew who he was even though it had been a long time since I'd seen him. His hesitation told me he wasn't sure. So, I helped him, "I'm the Irish Wop."

He says, "Oh, my God."

This was a long time later and I said, "But the name I use now is my real name. I'm Roberta Linn."

And he said, "I want you to call me when you get back to L.A. at Warners."

Well, I never called. Because, I thought it was just a moment of having drinks at the party and so on. Plus, I didn't want him to be embarrassed and feel bad or make myself feel bad. Then, when I told my mother she encouraged me to call him. "Get on the phone right now and call him," she said.

So, I called Mervyn at Warner Brothers studio and he said, "Where the hell have you been? I've been looking all over for you."

I didn't want to corner him. So, I left him an avenue for apology, "I thought maybe you'd just had a few drinks and it was just one of those moments where it was right for me to sound good to you."

He said, "No. You'll be just perfect for this. Come out and test for the part."

So, I went there, did my test, and guess who's going to be the leading man. It's Paul Newman. I said, "I'll do it for nothing." – Ha!

I can't think of the man who was the head of the casting, but he took one look at me and he heard me sing. I sang "Can't Help Lovin' that Man of Mine" and he said, "You are Helen Morgan."

So, I thought I had the part. When all of the sudden, Helen Morgan's mother decides she doesn't like the script. She thought it made her daughter look bad. After way too much legal process, LeRoy dumps the project but he passes me on to the next producer and director, on and on, until I finally got a screen test, and they tested me the same day as Anne Bancroft along with several other people. At this point, the fellow who was producing the movie was crazy about Ann Blythe, so Ann Blythe, who doesn't sing at all like Helen Morgan, got the part. But, it was funny that Mervyn LeRoy and I kept seeing each other over the years.

I worked in movies until I reached that awkward age when I wasn't small enough to play kids parts and I wasn't a woman yet either. That's when I really started singing with bands. But, by the time I was thirteen years old, I looked older and I won a contest to sing with Sterling Young and his Orchestra. I was already a pretty seasoned entertainer. I'd done a lot of singing, acting and dancing; I'd done a lot of shows. The contest was at the Aragon ballroom in Southgate and I got the job to sing with the band during summer vacation.

I don't remember a whole bunch about the contest except I remember my shoes. My mother had bought me these primo high heels and they were so pretty. I was so thrilled with those shoes. There were a lot of kids there, a lot of them older than I was. But, I sang well. I had good pitch, good sound, good phrasing and good timing. I sang more like a woman than a little girl.

Working for Sterling was interesting. He was a commercial band, a hotel band. But, when I could, I used to sneak into and sing at some of the Jazz clubs, even with some of the black groups like the Honey Drippers. I was too young to go myself. So, I would dress up and I'd get my cousin Dora Lou to take me into these clubs. I had to have somebody older with me so I could sneak in and sing. These clubs were all over L.A on Manchester Boulevard and Hollywood. Their names are hard to remember but I think one was called the Flame.

These were small clubs where these little groups worked around at all these Jazz places. Vido Muso, who played with the Stan Kenton Band would sing songs like, "Nothing Till You Hear From Me," and he played a fabulous rendition of "Sorrento." Later, he became my mother's God-father.

I only worked for Sterling Young for a short time, because about this time my mother had an opportunity to go into the service. But not before I had my first love.

Growing up in Huntington Park, I had my first crush and first kiss, while I was living with my Grandma. He was going to Huntington Park High school. I was in Junior High.

His name was Harold Shell and he had a candy apple red Ford coupe with twin pipes on it and lots of chrome. Boy, was he cute. You could hear his car coming three blocks away.

There was a Clock Drive-in, like in those fifties movies where all the guys and gals lined up in their cars and went, "Vroom, Vroom, Vvroom." We'd go to the drive-in and he'd be revving his engine. I thought I'd died and gone to heaven with this guy.   After a movie, one night, he brought me home and we had no idea what trouble awaited us. My Grandmother was real strict and you didn't even say darn in the house. It was too close to damn. She'd sit in the dark in her living room, in this little court apartment, and the door had French doors with little glass panes.

When Harold brought me home, he walked me to the door and my back is leaning against the wall. He had his arm up over me, leaning on his elbow, and he's just about to give me a kiss, "my very first kiss," and an arm comes out from around the door and it's my Grandma. She grabs me around the neck and pulls me in.

Well, Harold took off like a bat out of hell and my Grandmother drags me by the ear to my mother in the back bedroom so she can declare, "Madge, Madge. You better come out here and talk to this girl because she's out there mooching on the front door step." Not smooching, Mooching.

It was the funniest thing as I think back now.

Harold, took off in his car. I didn't see him again for a month.

Eventually, he went off to join the Army and became a paratrooper. Then, in the mid 1990's, I was singing in the city of Downey, doing a concert in the park, and some man comes up and says, "Remember me?"

Well, he didn't look anything like he did on the front porch when I knew him

He said, "It's Harold."

I said, "Harold Shell?"

He said, "Yeah." Of course, he had his wife with him and this was only four or five years ago. You could have knocked me over with a feather. But, it was nice seeing him again. Oh, I had such a crush on him. He was my first boyfriend and my first kiss. He was special. He passed away in 1997.

Sad Sack of the WAC'S

We were having a hard time financially and my mother had the chance to go into the service as a legal secretary. Bill had already gone off into the Army, he was seventeen or eighteen years old. So, it was just mom and I. My mom and dad had long since divorced. I don't remember why my mom and dad divorced; it was too painful to remember.

I was going to Saint Mary's Academy at the time, studying with this little Catholic nun and Mom was working down at Bethlehem Steel Yards as an executive secretary. She had this opportunity to go into the Army and thought it would be good but she didn't know what to do with me. So she was going to leave me in this Catholic school, in the convent, and I started pleading with my mother, "Please Mom, don't go. Don't leave me!"

Now, remember, I was only thirteen but I could pass for eighteen or twenty years old and you had to be eighteen to go in the Army. So, I kept pleading with my mother, "Take me with you!"

Finally, exasperated, she shot back, "What am I going to do? I've got a chance to make enough money to keep you in school. Bill's in the Army and we don't have anybody to leave you with but your Grandmother." Whom

19

Roberta Linn

MINE EYES HAVE SEEN THE GLORY

WOMEN'S ARMY CORPS

There is a controversy over this poster. I believe this is me. While on KP duty one day, I was cleaning the Officer's Club grease trap when I was called to pose for this. The women's Army Corps denies it's me. But it does look like me, doesn't it?

20

I loved very much, but she was not in the best of health.

I persisted, "Let me go with you."

She said, "Are you crazy?"

"No mom let me try. Let me try" and just like that she gave in. I joined the WAC's, passed the entry tests and physicals, and ended up going into the Army with my mother. I was nearly fourteen when I entered and ended up performing two years of service to my country. I was in the Woman's Army Corps earning a salary and took the train from Los Angeles to Des Moines, Iowa, where mom and I did our Basic Training.

I was the Sad Sack of the Army. I was just a kid. It was hard to keep up. We had to have everything folded just so in the foot lockers and my mother was constantly getting me up and helping get me ready. We had Colonel Oveta Culp, who wasn't the head of the Army, but she was definitely in charge of us. She came in for white glove inspections and made us parade. We did a lot of marching and I did it well. I had great timing learned from all my singing and dancing.

One particular morning we had an inspection and I was in a rush to get ready. We had to dress in uniform, and in my hurry to get my locker ready, I didn't have time to put on my garter belt to hold my stockings up. So, I had my socks stuck in my bloomers which I wore for calisthenics. I had my boots on and my jacket plus an overcoat, because it was very cold in Iowa, and my cute little pill box hat and my gloves, but I didn't have a garter belt and when we get right in front of the reviewing stand it happened; my stockings fell down over my shoes. Not only was it embarrassing, but I was put on permanent KP duty for the rest of the time I was in Basic Training.

Oh, it was awful. My mother could have killed me. I was on guard duty at night, I had to clean the grease traps in the kitchen, which was an awful mess.

My redemption was when they found out I could sing. They started using me for recruiting and then shipped me off to San Francisco's Fort Ord. By the time World War II was nearing its end I'd switched coasts to New York City with ten people working for me, doing embarkation files and recruiting.

When you sign up to go in the service they want to know, what are your capabilities? What do you do? Are you good at office work? Can you type? I did some typing I was pretty good, having learned at school. But the big thing was that I was an entertainer. The good stuff started happening when I was transferred to New York and they saw on my papers that I could sing. They were looking for a singer to sing with an Army band.

I was working at the Port of Embarkation as my main job, but New York was also home to the U.S. Army band. All the famous guys like Walter Gross (a great song writer), Sy Oliver (who arranged orchestras), Buddy Marino (a big band singer), and others were there. All these guys didn't want to go over and fight, so the Army put them together in a band and we did all the big Army Radio shows that were broadcast overseas to the service people all around the world.

They still didn't know my age. But, they kept interrogating me all the time. My mother was now at Fort Lee, Maryland. We were closer to each other once we were both on the same coast. San Francisco was so far away. They wanted my mother so bad because of all her secretarial skills. At this time, she was doing some of the minutes for the Nuremburg trials, with the Italian and Germans. She was taking the minutes for the depositions.

I even have an address book that is written in German from one of the Nazi soldiers with Goebbels telephone number in it. I also have a swastika silver coin with Hitler's picture on it; a gift from one of my mothers interviewees.

Champagne Lady

I was in the Army for two years and yes, I had all the kid diseases. I had the measles and the mumps and was eventually shipped over to Fort Lee, Maryland, with my mom, where I was hospitalized. Then finally, I got discharged.

THERE IS A LIGHT

There is a light shining through my window,
Oh yes, It is the sun!

I hear a bird singing just outside,
A new day has begun!

Oh, that I can see that light
And hear that song bird sing!

Just stop and think when you're feeling low
What a brand new day can bring

Roberta Linn
January, 1988

California Here We Come

After I was brought back to Fort Lee, Maryland, I remember driving back across country with mother in an old Ford and when we got to Prescott, Arizona the war was over. It was announced on the radio and there was screaming and hollering, people were dancing in the streets. We got out and celebrated with everybody.

We didn't have much to show for ourselves after our time in the Army. But, after spending a night in Prescott, we made it on into Los Angeles and stayed with my Grandmother, my mother's mother, Dora Bristow, in Huntington Park.

Before we got settled to well in Southern California, my mother was offered what she thought was a great job back in Texas. She left me with Grandma to try this opportunity, but before too long she was swindled. I can remember my mother started a business in Dallas, Texas, with some friends and they politely took all her money and left her stranded there. I was in a girl's school, San Marino Hall, back in California.

Due to my Mother's experience at Bethlehem Steel, she thought she could sell home garage welding machines. Her friends, the Holts, had picked up the distributor shift for Texas. But, after she got down there, went on the road and was selling these things, her friends took all the money. They took all the checks and cashed them but never paid her a cent. Then one night they just disappeared.

I got on a train to go and help momma, because I could make some good money singing. I did look a good deal older than I was and had no trouble getting jobs. Plus, it was summer vacation and it was a good time to go.

When I got there I found my mother living in this little motel, they'd taken all her money. So, I went to the MCA office, Music Corporation of America, in Dallas and asked if there were any openings for singers; could I get a job? They told me about this little territory band with a Canadian band leader made up of about twelve musicians with one-nighters booked across Louisiana and Texas. We got down to this small town in Louisiana, we'd done our one-nighter. She'd hid all the money we'd been paid for our singing that night under our mattress in the motel. It was the kind of place where each room was its own individual teeny tiny cabin. Also, we'd left behind all our clothes, costumes and music. We went to get a hamburger in momma's Ford and on the way back all the stoplights turned on. We could hear a fire engine siren. I looked at my mom and said, "Wow. What a wonderful day for a weenie bake."

I didn't realize it was our cabin that was burning down. I think maybe somebody robbed us that night, took the money and burnt it down to destroy the evidence. For a moment, I thought I could rush in and save some of our stuff. But, a fireman tackled me, it wasn't safe and thank God he did. The place was roaring bigger than a college bonfire. I'll never forget, as long as I'll live; we had no money, I had no music, I had no gowns and we were stranded in this little town without a toothbrush and just the clothes on our back.

The people in the town felt sorry for us. There was this man who had this nightclub in the heart of this town. It was an awful joint. All the soldiers from a nearby camp would come in and flick cigarettes at me. But, the piano player was magnificent, although an alcoholic. So, I'd just stand in the middle of this bar, singing my songs, and pray. We were just singing for our meals. They put us up in this roachy motel, and of course, they'd charge us for it. Everything I made went to put a roof over our head.

The piano player we met though was a great musician out of New York who was also down on his luck, stuck down there, and then matters got worse. Our car was parked out front and somebody cut our tires so it wasn't drivable. Now we didn't have any tires and we didn't have any money. Luckily, the piano player had gotten a job to play a gig in Lake Charles, Louisiana and told us the band was looking for a girl singer. Then he offered, "If I can get some tires for you and you drive my wife and me to Lake Charles. You'll have a job." We made it to Lake Charles, but not before we had another bad turn. We ran out of money in another little town before we made it and this one had a Quonset hut doubling as a bar and a bingo parlor. We walked in and there was this old piano. Our friend the piano man sat down and started playing and I started singing Stormy Weather. The guy who owned the place came over and said, "If you'll sing it again, I'll give you twenty bucks."

I said, "Twenty dollars?" We were busted. The guy and his wife with us were broke also. It was an offer I'm still thankful for. I must have sang Stormy Weather fifty times, I think. This guy kept doling out money and I kept singing. It got us a motel room, it got us dinner and it got us to Lake Charles.

In Lake Charles, we worked a bingo hall. Bingo was very big back there then. Our luck changed when momma bought a bingo ticket. She won $500 on this ticket. I left the band, we got in the car and just made it back to L.A. on her winnings.

Mom went back to work again with Bethlehem Steel yards as an executive secretary and I was picking up little gigs around while trying to get an education. My education was pretty spotty. But, I did finally graduate.

I was pretty smart. I mean, think I was. You know some people talk about street smarts. I had grown up around adults. I was way ahead of my years, I think. I was fifteen going on thirty.

I started singing around and got a job at a place where they had strippers. I'll never forget it as long as I live. It was called the Malibar club and they had a Jazz band and I knew the guys in the band. So, I got the job. I didn't even know there were strippers in there until my mother came in and saw what it was. I can still remember her pulling me by the ear out the back door. That was too bad, because it paid pretty good and the band was wonderful. But, I didn't know. I had no idea. I was just a singer with the band in between shows. I only worked there about a week. I don't think I even realized what was going on. I was so young. I guess I was still very naïve in a lot of ways.

Luckily, I'd never gotten into any trouble with my personal life. It was funny because I was still a kid in a lot of ways, a lot of little kid things still came out of me, but never any personal problems. I never got into any problems with any men sexually while in the Army. I was lucky. There could have been a lot of problems.

I also started plugging songs for Chappelle Music. Chappelle Music was one of the largest music publishing houses in the world. I remember one of the songs that I did. Ginny Simms had a radio show on CBS in Hollywood and I also did the morning show called the Breakfast Club out of Chicago plugging songs on there. The publishers would give you money to go on the show and plug their songs, like on the Ginny Simms show. I introduced a song called "Symphony" that later Joe Stafford recorded. But, I did it the very first time it was ever on radio.

The idea of plugging songs was there were a lot of good radio shows playing live music. There were all kinds of shows coming out of Hollywood and L.A. and my agent would get a spot on the show for me to sing the song with an introduction like, "...and now Roberta Linn will sing Symphony." I'd be the guest and go on and sing a song. Then the publisher would give me the rate pay. I'd just show up, see the song written and the publisher would make his money, royalties, for each performance, plus the music lead sheets.

The man I'd learn the songs from, his name was Jack Carrol. He was the piano player at Chappelle music. In the old days, they always had a piano player in the studio who played the songs for people so they could introduce songs to the big singers, the artists, repertoire men from the big record companies, or band leaders. They'd bring us a lot of songs. Sometimes I even got a few beautiful gifts from some of the big time song writers like Jimmy McHugh, who wrote" I'm in the Mood for Love."

Jimmy McHugh went with Louella Parsons, the big columnist out of Hollywood, and I was at her house several times, placed upon the piano to sing some of Jimmy's songs. She had these absolutely gorgeous parties at her house. All the movie stars would come; Kim Novak, Jimmy Stewart, George Jessel, Rhonda Fleming. All of Hollywood was there, all the big stars, it was great to be an invited guest. Jimmy would get me up on the piano and I would sing his songs. But, I was a guest. I wasn't hired. I was still pretty young, but I looked older.

About this time, I auditioned for a fellow by the name of Sam Lutz, who's office had Liberace, Lawrence Welk, Frankie Lane, and other great musicians and singers. Davey, Lutz and Heller were a big management team and had one of the largest musical stable of talent in the industry at the time.

When I auditioned for Sam and I hadn't quite graduated high school yet and gotten my credits. He said, "Boy, I really like the way you sing. How old are you?"

I told him I was twenty.

He said, "No, you're not twenty. Are you out of school yet, finished high school?"

I fessed up and admitted I hadn't.

He said, "Well, when you finish high school come back and see me. You're too young for me to place with the bands or anything I have. I can't even put you under contract yet."

A year later, at seventeen, I ran into him over on Sunset Boulevard, while I was plugging a song again for Chappelle music.

He asked, "Are you out of school yet?"

I lied, "Yeah."

Then he answered, "Lawrence Welk is looking for a Champagne Lady."

I said, "What the heck is a Champagne Lady and who is Lawrence Welk?" I'd never heard of him. Ray McKinley, Harry James, Les Brown them I knew, but Lawrence Welk? Who the heck was that?

I later learned he was very big in the mid-west. He was more of a commercial band, then Mr. Lutz continued, "He's going to be at the Hollywood Paladium tonight. He's looking for a girl singer and I think you'd be perfect. But, don't tell him you're seventeen. Tell him twenty." He guessed right at my true age.

Now remember, this is when the Paladium was the place to go. The big names played there, like Count Basie, Woodie Herman, and Stan Kenton. All the good bands played at the Hollywood Paladium. It's right on Sunset across from Earl Carroll's supper club, which became the

Moulin Rouge.

I called my mom to help get me there but in those days you didn't have the freeways from Huntington Park to get over to Hollywood. But she still said, "OK." It was early afternoon and she picked me up, first driving me back to Huntington Park so I could get all dolled up. Mom fixes my make-up and places my hair on top of my head, puts my little high heeled shoes on that I felt so glamorous in, and we drive all the way back to the Hollywood Paladium.

We get there about seven o'clock. There must have been three hundred girl singers in this place. There were more girl singers in there than dancers and nobody knew who Lawrence Welk was. This was before the TV show.

The dance floor was down in front and you had to go up four or five stairs to get to the outer room where all the tables and the bars were. That's where everybody sat and mom and I were at the last table kind of up against the stage.

Now these gals, he had every girl singer around, sang every song I had planned. In my head I'm thinking, Oh man, this is a total loss. It finally gets to about twelve thirty in the morning and the manager of the Paladium comes up and says, "Larry, if you audition one more girl singer tonight, you can take your accordion and your bubble machine and go back to Yankton."

We could hear this because we were right next to the stage. Well, my mother got worried, "Oh my God. We've been here since seven o'clock Roberta. I don't care if you don't get the job. You go up and tell him, 'Look, My mother is going to kill me if don't get to sing one song and tell him that Sam sent you."

So, I walked up and I tapped him on the shoulder and I said, "Mr. Welk, my name is Roberta Linn and my mom and I came all the way from Huntington Park. We've been sitting here since seven o'clock and these girls you

31

have sang every song. Mr. Lutz sent me and my mother said, 'if I don't sing one song she's going to kill me."

He started laughing and with his accent said, "Vat did ju say jor name vas?"

And I repeated, "My name is Roberta Linn."

He said, "Ruperta Linn," with one finger on his chin. "That's a very nice name kid. I hope you can sing."

I knew he liked the way I looked, I could tell. I was dressed real cute and demure, pretty. So, he said, "Sing a song. Vat are ju going to sing?"

Well, I sang "Embraceable You" and got in and I could tell he liked my singing.

Then he said, "Do ju know 'I'ma in love wid a wunnerful guy?"

This was a thrilling request, I had just learned this song. "Yes, Mr. Welk," I said, "I do know it." It's the one that goes:

> I'm as corny as Kansas in August
> I'm as normal as Blueberry pie

It was a big song.

So, he said, "Well Ruperta, the banda playsa four bar intro. You sing a chorus. The bandsa going to playa half a chorus. Youa come in. You go out. I'll showa you how to geta out of de song."

I said, "Ok Mr. Welk." So, the band played the four bars, I got in. The key was perfect. The band played a half a chorus, I came in right on the button and finished with the band and about one o'clock in the morning, after all these girls singing, he looked at me and said, "Youa know Ruperta, youa are the new Champagne Lady."

I got the job! This was on a Thursday night. I was in tears and I said, "Well, my mom's not going to kill me now." I got the job!

I did my first recording session with the Welk band on Sunday at Mercury records. Mitch Miller was the artist and repertoire man and I sang and recorded "A Dream is a Wish Your Heart Makes" and "Bibbity Bopity Boo" from Cinderella.

The day after that, on Monday, we left on a cross country tour for Miller High Life Beer.

This was a small postcard used for marketing and
publicity of Lawrence Welk and his Champagne
Orchestra from the Aragon Ballroom.

The Star of the Welk Era

On Monday, we packed up and left on the road in a fleet of cars. We were under contract from Miller High Life Beer. "The Champagne of Bottled Beer with Champagne Music" and we had to be in a different city each time we did a show. We did 42 weeks of one-nighters before we had a day off and averaged three hundred miles a day. We slept in our cars some nights, slept on couches in hotel lobbies at others and ate greasy spoons. We were on the full ABC Radio network and did all the Miller High Life commercials where the low voice did "MILLER" and I was (high tone) "High Life." (low) "Miller" (high) "High Life. The Champagne of Bottled Beer."

Then we worked our way back to the coast and opened at the Aragon Ball Room on Lick Pier at Ocean Park, California. We had about ten couples in the ballroom that evening. I'll never forget it. The whole band had a meeting and we decided we're not going back on the road again. So, everybody quit.

And, it just so happened that KTLA, which was the big television station in LA at the time, channel 5, was interested in us. It was the Paramount studios station and the man running the station was named Klaus Landsberg. He was brilliant. He did all the big musical shows. He did

35

Roberta Linn

This photo was taken when I was seventeen and used as
a glamour shot for Lawrence Welk.
Do you think I could get into a nightclub?

the Spade Cooley show, Harry Owens and the Royal Hawaiians with Hula Hattie and they shot it from the Aragon ballroom. They would shoot it off the back of the pier so it looked like it was in Hawaii, complete with the Hawaiian sets.

Well, Mr. Landsberg loved our band and he was from Germany. He'd left as the important German immigrant, who developed the color tube for RCA. They'd brought him to the states when he was 16 or 17 years old and RCA didn't live up to their contract with him. So, he ended up in California with Paramount studios to start an experimental station that ended up being KTLA.

Being from Germany he loved our Viennese waltzes, he loved our Polkas, and he said Lawrence (Welk), "I'll tell you what. I'll put you on a Wednesday night following the Harry Owens show. It'll be from 10 till 11" and the Harry Owens show was a big show at that time.

Now the band was still on strike, we're not going back on the road. We're too worn out from doing all those one-nighters.

Mr. Lawrenberg said, "I'll split it with you. I'll pay for a half hour, if you (Welk) will pick up the other half hour. I'll coast ya and we'll see if we can pick up a sponsor."

Well, our first sponsor was City Chevrolet and I introduced a song:

See the USA in your Chevrolet...

That was my song. It turned out to be Dinah Shore's later. But that was my song. It was written for me. It was:

Buy your Chevrolet at City Chevrolet...

Then we got Chicken of the Sea Tuna and Laura Scudder Potato Chips. Those were our first commercial sponsors for the Lawrence Welk show and they helped get the momentum really swinging.

We went from ten couples in the ballroom in August to, by the time New Year's Eve rolled around, a full house,

Mr. Welk had this great gimmick he'd use to get people involved. At some point during the show, he'd invite the audience onstage to dance with any of the musicians they wanted, including me.

you couldn't get in the Aragon. It was so packed with people,...the television show took off like,... I use the old phrase... Buster's Gang. Unbelievable. The fellas had to lift me up over the stage to get me back to my dressing room to the ladies room. I couldn't get off the stage. I signed autographs until I had blisters on my fingers. I couldn't go on the freeways without people honking their horns at me or following me around the markets. It was incredible. Six months of television did that for Lawrence Welk and for me too.

When we were at the Aragon, mom and I were living in an apartment in Santa Monica on Seventeenth Street and I had a little Chihuahua I loved desperately. She could sing "Momma's Little Baby Loves Shortcake." She could talk. I had her on the Larry Finley show and the Welk show. That dog could say MAMA as plain as any baby. One day, we were at rehearsal and Rocky Rockwell, who was the trumpet player with the band, he was doing the Jazz version of, "Mama's little baby loves shortening, shortening," and all of the sudden, Chiquita starts saying, "Mam, MA, Mama, Rawa, Mama."

Lawrence looked at me and I looked at him. My mother started laughing. I mean we'd had her talking in the car a little bit, but nothing like this. She liked to say Mama, Mama. As a result, we had her on the TV show and she actually sang with Rocky. It was so funny. She sang, "Mama, Rawa, Mam, ma, Mara. Rama, Mama." Every time I'd say Mama, she'd repeat it.

We were living in this apartment, my mother, my dog Chiquita and myself. I was taking schooling on the side. I was tutored and had some private schools. Later on, I did try and go to a City College but, I couldn't, I just couldn't. I tried for about two years and in the end there was just too much going on in my life.

A surprise 19th birthday party thrown for me at the Aragon Ballroom. There were 250 cakes prepared to serve all the guests

My mother was very talented and we made Valances for the windows. It was really pleasant because we had a nice place to live in now and could stay for a while. My mother was a beautiful woman, she was absolutely gorgeous. I remember seeing a picture of her sitting on a horse bareback with a long black braid of hair, a beautiful high forehead and a sharp nose. She had some Indian blood in her. I think of her as a beautiful Pocahontas. She was absolutely gorgeous.

When I was with Welk, I met a wonderful gentleman who was a big fan of mine. His name was Robert Amour and he ran the Ford plant in Wilmington. He just loved the Welk band and he loved my singing. We did a big show for him and at one point I mentioned, "I sure would like to have my own car."

So, he ran a car through his production line for me. It was like custom built. A Ford Fairlaine with white on the outside and a powder blue interior. It was so cute and I thought I was so special. It was so nice of Mr. Amour to do that for me.

We did a lot of shows in the nearby cities on our days off from the Aragon and we stayed in the Aragon ballroom for years. Then overlapping my time with Welk, I started my own TV show.

KTLA was owned by Paramount studios. So, whenever I needed any clothing for the Welk show I'd go over and pick out from all the costume department; the same thing for my show. I actually wore a gown on Café Continental that Marlene Dietrich wore in a movie called Golden Earrings or something.

At one point, I was on every magazine cover you can imagine. I was on the cover of TV and Radio Life, Peo-

Harry Gosling, Garth Andres, Curt Ramsey, also known as The Sparklers, with Lawrence Welk and myself. I often performed in duets, quartets and with other people while working for Welk. This was for our Moonlit Bay album.

ple magazine (did a great story), TV and Radio Mirror, everything. There was a columnist with the Daily News newspaper named Paul Prace and I think I was in his column everyday. I was doing interviews on the radio stations constantly and while I was on staff at CBS and NBC while doing the Welk show with the ABC Netwrok Live. Plus I was doing the voices on Frosty Follies, which was a beautiful Ice Capades show that Klaus put on the air, and don't forget I was doing my own show too. My days and nights had suddenly seemed to never end from activity.

One day, I couldn't get out of bed. I was so tired. I couldn't lift my arms and legs and they rushed me to the hospital. I was very young and I was totally exhausted.

Mr. Welk didn't understand. The only thing important to him was the band and the show.

I was a workaholic and when I ended up in the hospital the Welk band had a show to do in Ventura. Klaus said, "You can't go. You've got to stay here and get your rest." He tried talking to Mr. Welk but it was no use. Lawrence said, if I didn't make it, he'd have to find somebody else.

I couldn't believe it. After all those years, all the hard work, the long shifts, the nights of little sleep, the countless events and everything and he just didn't understand. I begged the doctor to get me on my feet. I was afraid of losing my job. So, they gave me some dexadrines, put me in a whirlpool bath, got me up and out to do the shows. I did the Welk show. I did my show and I ended up in the hospital again.

Eventually, I went back. I was doing my show and his and he (Welk) was very callous in regards to anything slowing down the Orchestra. He just didn't want to understand I was very young and the physical things he was demanding of me were too much.

This photo was taken near ronald reagan's hometown, in Springfield, Illinois, with Lawrence Welk on the Miller High Life Beer tour. Reagan was asking me for a dance. Often people comment about how he was looking at me. But can you guess what I said by my expression?

This Chicago record store hosted one of my first record signing ceremonies.

KTLA took this shot in the early 1950's to promote
my show Cafe Continental.

Champagne Lady

LAWRENCE WELK FEATURING ROBERTA LINN
and his Champagne Music *"The Champagne Lady"*

APPEARING AT
Aragon Ball Room
LICK PIER — OCEAN PARK, CALIF.

This photo was staged. I was actually on a bench with
boards supporting my back and legs. The champagne
glass was super-imposed.

On a weekend away to relax with some much needed rest, I was staying at the Lake Arrowhead Hotel when I ran into Al Weil in the dining room and he recognized me. He came over and introduced himself, "Hi, I'm Al Weil, Rocky Marciano's manager."

I said, "I know Rocky." My dad had introduced me to him/ My dad had refereed some fights in the Olympic Auditorium, in Los Angeles when I was younger.

We hung out the whole time I wa at the Lake Arrowhead Hotel. The hotel had steam rooms, massages and baths. I needed the rest. Rocky was really working out getting ready for his fight with Sonny Liston.

A glamour shot from when I was under contract
with Paramount Studios.

I won the 1955 Emmy Award for my show Cafe Continental as the Most Outstanding Female Entertainer
on TV. The event was held at the Hollywood Paladium. It was like a cannon went off in my head when
I heard my name called out.

At a Palm Springs party with Bing crosby everyone had to dress Hawaiian. I remember that Angie Dickinson was there too. I had the great honor of singing with Bing. It was so special.

I toured with Bob Hope in 1956 to help the foreign premieres of his movie *Eddie Foy and the Seven Little Foys*. I did Jane Russell's parts and played Bob's straight man as we toured through Australia, Southeast Asia, and Hawaii. He was the best teacher on comic timing and wonderful to work with.

Actor Richard Boone (of Paladin fame) and myself
at the Academy of Television and Radio Arts.
He was a fantastic date.

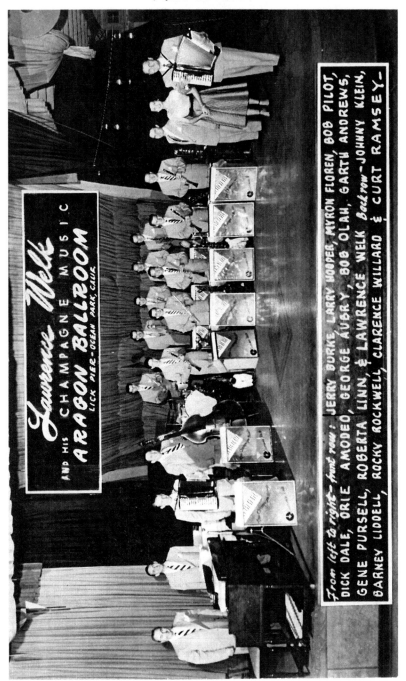

From left to right—front row: JERRY BURKE, LARRY HOOPER, MYRON FLOREN, BOB PILOT, DICK DALE, ORIE AMODEO, GEORGE AUBRY, BOB OLAH, GARTH ANDREWS, GENE PURSELL, ROBERTA LINN, & LAWRENCE WELK. Back row—JOHNNY KLEIN, BARNEY LIDDELL, ROCKY ROCKWELL, CLARENCE WILLARD & CURT RAMSEY.

The Lawrence Welk Orchestra at the height of its inception into television. It was this band which originally made Lawrence Welk a national household name.

Garth Andrews

Orie Amodeo

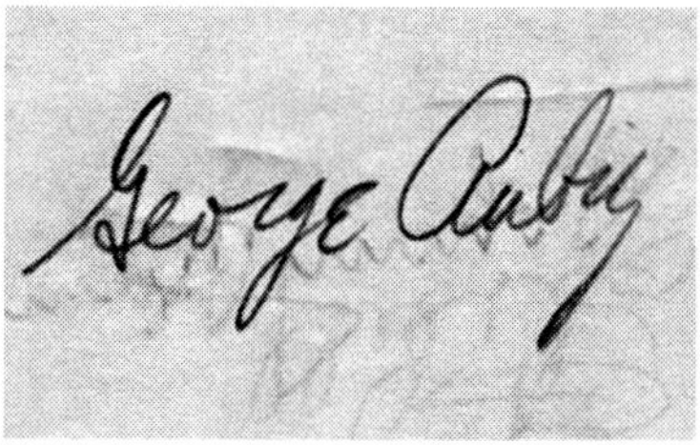

George Aubry

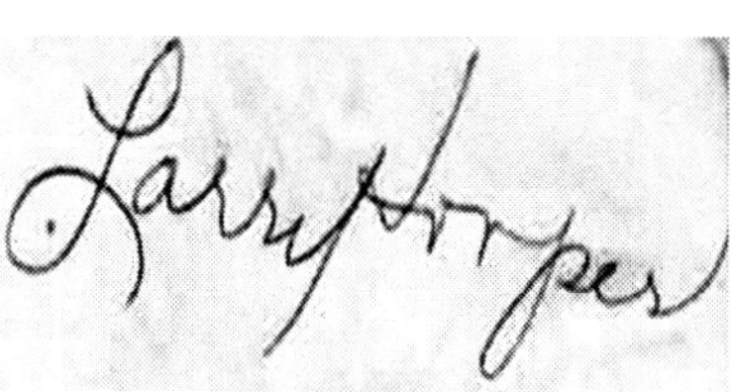

Jerry Burke

Dick Dale

Myron Floren

Larry Hooper

Johnny Klein

I've kept every one of these signatures in my personal autograph book for over fifty years.

Barney Liddell

Bob Olah

Bob Pilot

Gene Pursell

Curt Ramsey

Rocky Rockwell

Lawrence Welk

Clarence Willard

The Champagne Glass Cracks

I'm very near sighted, so I couldn't read cue cards. Therefore, I memorized the songs for all the shows. I had to memorize five or six songs a week. On top of that, I was doing all the voices for Frosty Follics, on Wednesday nights. Then, when I'd finish that show, they'd have my little Fairlaine running outside of the Ice skating rink and I'd literally jump in my car and drive all the way down to Santa Monica by myself, so I could be there on time for my spot with ABC National Radio and the Lawrence Welk band. I'd work for him until two o'clock in the morning and if he had a recording session the next day, or a record signing, you know, or if we had to open a Sears and Roebuck store, I'd have to be up at eight or nine o'clock in the morning to go do those things. After all that, I'd have to rest just a little bit and go back to sing till two o'clock in the morning again.

Plus, there was my show on Tuesdays, Café Continental, named for the commissary at Paramount studios, which was sponsored by the Gas Appliance Dealers of America, it was a great syndicated show.

I had all kinds of wonderful entertainers on the show: Marge and Gower Champion, and dancers from the Bolshoi ballet, Josh White, Josephine Premice, John St. Blon. I had the Melon Men on there singing as waiters who did the commercials for:

"Use Ajax, the Foaming Cleanser
A Tiger in Your Tank."

The show had to be entirely different from what I did with Welk. I couldn't do the same types of songs I did for him. Because, it would have been a no no.

While working for Welk I was paid One Hundred and Twenty Five dollars a week from Welk in the beginning and it stayed that way till after my television show. I think I was making a Hundred and Fifty dollars a week when I won the Emmy award in 1954. It was scale. He just didn't pay very much money.

When I finally left the band, he wanted me to sign a Hollywood movie loan out contract. Studios, like Warner Brothers, would sign stars to these and then they could loan out actors to other studios, like Paramount. But, Warner would get all the money Paramount paid for the star and whatever the star signed for with Warner is what they would get. If Paramount gave them a million dollars and Warner was giving the star $25,000 then Warner made the rest of it. That's what Lawrence wanted me to sign.

Well, my mother didn't feel the contract was fair. Because at that point, I was getting to be a pretty big star, I was on my way up. So, we finally got an attorney to try and negotiate a nice contract. I wasn't asking for anything too big, but so I had some sort of graduating scale and was getting compensated. I thought, Boy, I'm going out and doing all kinds of shows and getting $150 a week with Lawrence Welk. No matter what he got. There had to come a time when Roberta Linn was going to make some more money. I mean, I couldn't stay at the same pay point forever.

Just when things seemed like they might be straightened out it got into a bad thing, a very sad situation. I came on the show one night and live on TV, without any warning, Lawrence said, "Ruperta, don't ja tink ja ott to tell the folks jor going to leave da band."

I didn't know he was going to do that. I started to cry and I looked at him, "What is he doing to me?" I really loved my spot on the Lawrence Welk show. The fans were wonderful and he broke my heart the night on live TV, when he announcedmy departure without me knowing. It was like a lightning bolt hit me and it broke my heart because I really loved what I did for Mr. Welk and I worked very hard for him.

Then, I had to stay on the band for about thirty days while he auditioned. It was tough. All the lovely people who became so close as fans and friends would come to me and ask, why was I leaving? And, I wasn't allowed to answer. I mean, this is the first time I've really talked about it. But he was really… I mean to do something like that to me was awful. I worked so hard for him and he just didn't ... Mr. Welk was like a really proud German father and when he couldn't get his own way, when something got in the way of the progress of the Orchestra, this was how he got back at me. He made me watch while he was auditioning other people for my part and I was heart broken.

Eventually though, it came to it's end.

I stayed on my own show, Café Continental, for another 2 years but then Klaus died very young of cancer.

I was offered a contract to sign with MCA; they were a huge big booking agency. I can remember going to this big office with this very handsome man sitting behind this huge desk made of deep dark wood. He offered a great contract, but my mother said we should turn it down. BIG MISTAKE. The deal was several thousand dollars up front to come with them. I was on my way up at this time and it was huge signing bonus. They would have kept me on retainer until they found me a movie, a recording contract or something.

It's the one time in my life where I can say where my mother made a bad decision. I should have signed. It would have been a good step in my career, because they were big enough to overcome anything Welk would do. For years it was difficult. He (Welk) really tried to hurt my career. I couldn't record for another two years after I left him and there was a lot of things that went along with that.

After Klaus died, I really lost it, as far as the TV show went. He'd been my mentor. He was a good friend and without him my show didn't feel right and I became very depressed.

I still miss Klaus Landsberg. Did you know, he's the one who got on the top of the mountains to set up the relays to film the atomic bomb testings in Nevada? He was able to capture the filming of that and then he died of cancer at an early age. He was about thirty nine years old when he died. I really looked up to him because he was talented and so kind to me. He boosted my career whenever he could.

And I still miss Lawrence Welk too. All the wonderful musicians, the fans from the Welk show, Mr. Welk and the times we got along and that great band that started a show lasting thirty years on television. We, all of us involved in those early formulative years, working hard as a group, made it all happen. Wow, what a team! And what a great pleasure it was to be a part of it all as the first TV Champagne Lady. We were the reason the band and the show went national.

RX: LAUGHTER

Laughter is one medicine
They can't put into pills,
But, somehow a little laughter
can cure a million ills.

So, a prescription just for you I'll write.
RX: Laughter before breakfast
Laughter before lunch,
And laughter before you sleep at night

Be sure to increase your dose each day,
And you're sure to feel better right away.

Roberta Linn
January, 1988

Not Now Lord,
I've Got Too Much To Do

When Klaus died and I didn't go with MCA, I signed with the William Morris agency and went to work Las Vegas. I opened at the New Frontier Hotel and Casino co-headlining with Marge and Gower Champion. Nelson Riddle did my music, Edith Head did my gowns, Charlie O'Curran staged my act and it was a show stopper. It was fantastic. I closed with a medley of my Uncle's songs. Did I tell you that my uncle worked in the music department at Warner Brothers? That was how I got my first part in a movie at Warner Brothers, thanks to my uncle Al Dubin, who wrote the whole score for "Forty Second Street." He was the lyric writer.

So, Charlie had me in a big gown, then changing into a medium lenghth gown, to a leotard. I did a whole thing like a Judy Garland routine ending in a tuxedo with the hat and cane and I sang my uncle's songs. Dancing and singing to; "Dancing With a Tear in My Eyes," "I Only Have Eyes For You," "Forty Second Street," "Lullaby of Broadway," "Lulu's Back in Town," "Shuffle Off to Buffalo," these were all my uncle's lyrics.

I worked Nevada, seventeen years, at least forty-two to forty-nine weeks a year. I worked Reno and Tahoe

63

also, but my start was in Vegas. And occasionally I went out on the road.

I was supposed to have opened at the Sands hotel with Martin and Lewis. I was going to do a picture with them at Paramount Studios after Vegas, but I ended up with pneumonia in both lungs for the second time.

In fact, my first bought with pneumonia was here in Palm Springs. I was working the Chi Chi club, staying at the El Mirador hotel, that's when Ray Ryan owned it and Frank Bogert was General Manager. I woke up with 105 fever in my room and they rushed me to the hospital. I could hardly breathe and they gave me a series of anti-biotics which my mother and I later discovered can only be taken maybe every two or three years.

I was finally well enough after a few months and head off to Vegas for the show with Dean and Jerry. But, I'd gone back to work a little too soon. So, they rushed me off the Cedars and they gave me the anti-biotics again.

Well, my mother didn't know and neither did I that I shouldn't take this so soon. And nobody had informed the medical staff that I had been taking Chloromiceten. They darn near killed me with it. I blew up like a balloon. I couldn't eat. I couldn't eliminate. I had the biggest lab bill with Cedars that had been seen at the time.

The headlines in the newspapers said I was dying. The reporters on KTLA and holy rollers everywhere were saying prayers every hour for me. There were flowers all over the hospital from fans, friends and family.

Michael Montoya, a priest from the San Gabriel mission, whom I'd done a lot of benefits for, and practically helped him build his own chapel showed up. He was in the room with me when I was so sick, about three weeks into the treatment, I was dying. I blew up, my skin broke open, and I looked like I'd been in the oven too long, like a turkey.

I had an out of body experience. My mother was

leaning over me, saying, "Roberta, Roberta." I remember looking up on the ceiling and there was this bright light opening up like a tunnel. As I recall, I could see somebody's figure at the end of the tunnel but I couldn't see a face. My mother was crying and leaning over me and calling my name. Father Montoya was praying and holding my hand.

I remember, I was talking to my mother but she couldn't hear me. The doctors rushed in and I was having a heart attack. This was in 1958. They were working over me and working over me. They brought me back and then they called in the head of UCLA Medical, who said, "For God's sake, take this girl off all the medication."

What had happened was kind of gruesome sounding, but it's important to know. When I was on the anti-biotic I grew a fungus internally, in my system, just like on a lemon or a peach. It was in my mouth, so I couldn't swallow and I couldn't breathe. It was taking over my body.

It's a wonderful anti-biotic but it's also a very dangerous one. One of the doctors in Los Angeles had given this to his daughter and killed her. The doctor from UCLA Medical Clinic came to my rescue and ordered some kind of little pill to insert under my tongue. That probably was something to help fight the fungus or to help my heart and I was hooked up to all kinds of fluids and machines.

I was a year recuperating in my home in the Hollywood hills, up on Springhill Terrace which is right next to Griffiths Park. It was a lovely two story house and mother made me a bedroom out of the den.

Everybody in show business thought I was going to die.

There was a dear lady named Charlotte Rogers who did my publicity for a while when I worked in Vegas and on TV, One day she called to see how I was feeling.

I said, "Oh Charlotte, I gotta get back to work. I'm broke. I'm out of money."

She said, "You think you got trouble. Frank Sennis (Who owned the Moulin Rouge, formerly Earl Carroll's) lost the Ames brothers playing tonight. They had a fight and no one knows where they are. The press is set to show up and they don't have an act."

I saw this as an opportunity. I said, "Tell Frank I'll do it for nothing. Just give me the opportunity to get back in front of people and let them hear my sing. I've got to work. I'm desperate."

She said, "I think he's got Vic Damone."

I begged, "Please tell him. I'm really desperate. I need the job."

She called me back in a half an hour and said,"Grab your music and get down to the Moulin Rouge."

Springhill Terrace ran into Franklin which went straight down the hill to Sunset Boulevard, and I literally rolled down the hill to the club with my music and we rehearsed. My mom brought me my gowns down and made everything ready.

I opened. Well, nobody announced that the Ames Brothers weren't going to be there. They just introduced me and out I came.

I get goose bumps telling you this. I went over like, my favorite saying, Busters Gang. I was so glad to be back working and the band played my music great. Joey Stabile was the band leader. I got a standing ovation at the end of the show and Frank kept me on for the whole engagement. They put a big star on my dressing room that night and I got rave reviews from the press. It was so wonderful, Frank Sennis and his brother Rocky became my managers.

The Road to Vegas

Frank and Rocky Sennis took me under their wings and I starting working long term engagements. I went under contract with Karet Incorporated whoran the Desert Inn and the Stardust in Vegas. Through them I had a long term engagement at the Stardust and occasionally I'd go over and work at the Desert Inn with Jimmy Durante and other acts.

I worked back to back with Billy Daniels. Moe Dalite and Allen Rowan, people might know them from La Costa, that's the big golf resort on the west coast, they gave me a five year contract at the Stardust.

There was a huge showroom where the Lido show was performed. When the show would break, Billy and I would come out and do our own show. We held the people in the casino, for the gamblers. That was the whole idea of these big shows in Vegas, was to not let the people walk out the front door. So they stayed in the casino and played the tables.

When I wasn't working at the Stardust, they booked me in New York at the Copa Cabana and the Beverly Hills club, which was in Kentucky. That's where they had a terrible fire where John Davidson almost got killed. All the people couldn't get out and it was a huge fire. But luckily, I wasn't working there at the time.

Roberta Linn

All the big clubs, especially the gambling clubs were connected. I think of going back through into the Green felt Jungle, where they did the story about the people who ran Vegas. You know, the mafia, the mob connected people.

I worked for all of them. I worked in Chicago at the Living room. I worked at Manny Scars Sahara club. At Manny's Sahara club, Sam Giancanno, who was the head of Chicago used to come and watch us work all the time. For my birthday, there was this restaurant, called the Armory, where all the people who were connected used to go and eat. It was an Italian restaurant. I still have a necklace that Sam, they called him Moe, gave me, with the hunch-backed man and the horn and so on; heavy gold, when I was at the Armory having dinner.

There was Slicker Sam and his wife, who had an Italian restaurant, and Tommy MacDonald from Chicago. He was the host at the Stardust hotel in Vegas. He used to walk around with this little whistle.

I was there the night Sammy Davis came in with his entourage. You see, Vegas in the early days was very Jim Crow. The black entertainers weren't allowed to come into the casino or even eat in the restaurants. I was on stage when they threw him out of the hotel.

I was also at the Sands, working, when Lena Horne and Nat King Cole couldn't eat dining room. They had to eat in their suites and these were big big stars. They weren't allowed in the casino either.

Over the years of course, these things changed. I can honestly say that in my lifetime, I have been very blessed. I worked the best years of movies. I worked the best years of radio. I was on staff at NBC and CBS. I was on both networks that are doing the shows with Jay Leno now and the one that's doing David Letterman. But we were doing radio five days a week. I was in Vegas and I worked the big ballrooms. I worked the best years of the big band era. I worked just the tail end of it, but when the big ballrooms were just coming to their end.

What I did in my lifetime had brought me to the point of where I was in Vegas. I did all these wonderful things. I did movies. I did radio. I did the big band era. I did night-clubs when nightclubs were still there. I did television and it was from all of these things that I then leapt into Vegas. It was these experiences which put me into headlining on the strip.

It was at this same time when Elvis first appeared at the Frontier and bombed. Just prior to Marge Champion and me, he bombed out because it wasn't his crowd. He was too young. It was a different audience back then.

That's when Mario Lanza worked Vegas and he got so heavy because he was over eating. They had lots of problems with Mario Lanza; a lot of problems with Elvis Presley. But, at the New Frontier when Marge and Gower Champion and I opened with a thirty piece orchestra and fifty girls in a line, I mean when I was in Vegas it was the best years. All the high rollers were in. You'd think nothing of seeing someone getting a $5000 rack of $100 chips.

In Vegas, one of my highlights was when I worked with Danny Thomas at the Sands. Danny and I became very good friends. This was after I was so sick.

Jakie Friedman, who was head of the Sands hotel was the cutest little guy. You got to picture this: he had a Jewish accent and he was from Houston. So everything was, "Jou'all come to da Sands." From Houston he still had the Texas Y'all but he had a Jewish accent too. He wore a little Eisenhower jacket and a little golf cap and he just loved me. I thought he was just fantastic.

Then I worked the Shamrock hotel for Guy Mac-Carthy, who was a big oilman friend of Ray Ryan's, who I'll share a little bit of in the next chapter. That's the Shamrock Inn in Houston, a gorgeous gorgeous place.

Roberta Linn

I worked all the best placed thanks to Frank and Rocky Sennis and Ray Ryan, a special friend who helped get me my first gig in Vegas.

This photo was taken the night I met
Ray Ryan in Palm Springs.

A Man Comes Into My Life

The Ray Ryans of Palm Springs would be in Vegas also, and he was really responsible for my opening in Vegas at the new Frontier. Ray became a dear dear friend of mine. He owned the El Mirador and I met Ray when I was 18 years old and singing at the Tennis club, the one against the mountain, and they had $100 a plate dinner for cancer and Corinna Wright was the hostess. Dinah Shore was supposed to have done the show and for some reason she was sick and they called me and brought me in.

I came in, sang my songs, and this very handsome man came up to me after the show. He was gorgeous in his tuxedo and he said, "I love the way you sing. I would like to invite you to the El Mirador hotel. I'm having a party tonight."

I was only eighteen years old and my mother was always riding shotgun. My mom wouldn't let me go.

But then, the next morning, we were in this very nice motel, where they had us staying, and there comes a horn followed by a knock on the door. There's a gorgeous guy standing there in Levi's and cowboy boots, a country western shirt, with a 1950's Thunderbird behind him adorned with two horns on its hood. "How come you didn't come to my party last night?" he asks. "I wanted you to come and

I made the cover of *Palm Springs Villager* (now *Palm Springs Life*) in November 1955 when I was Queen of the Desert Circus Parade. Palm Springs was always my favorite place in the world, for many reasons, and still is today.

73

As Queen of the Desert Circus, I paraded on this horse down Palm Canyon Drive in a special pink leather outfit and hat. Later that day, I had one of my most embarrassing moments when I almost fell of the horse at the rodeo.

The time I came across Cary Grant while horseback riding in Palm Springs he was impeccably dressed; even his blue jeans were ironed. Notice that in this picture he is wearing cuff links.

Here I am skiing at lake Tahoe in Heavenly Valley while
working at the Sahara. I broke my leg this day against im-
plicit instructions in my contract which forbade me from
skiing. I lied and said I slipped on the ice in a parking lot
and finished out my contract singing from a barstool,
much to the frustration of my musicians.

I opened the Republican National convention in Chicago, Illinois with the Manny Harmon Orchestra. Mayor John Daly was the announcer. I sang a medley of Eisenhower's favorites and had to keep singing almost twenty minutes because the President was running late.

This was on the cover of *Television* magazine in the late 1950's and is one of my favorite photos.

This was taken at a solo performance in San Diego.
I always tried to give every one of my performances
everything I have, and still do.

I co-hosted the first Telethon for Multiple Sclerosis with Mickey Rooney. The show lasted 17 hours at the Ambassador Hotel in Los Angeles. I changed clothes every hour. This dress I'm wearing is the same one Jack Lemmon wore in *Some Like It Hot*.

I took this photo with my mom, Madge Hammond, during the 1960's in the Baccarat room at Caesar's Palace. My mom was my best friend and confidant. I owe the beginnings of my career to her.

meet all my friends."

"My mom wouldn't let me come."

"Well, I'm gonna take you horseback riding today."

"I don't have any clothes to go horseback riding. Mom, can I go horseback riding with Mr. Ryan?"

Over the top of my head he spoke to my mom from the doorway. He said, "Look, I think your daughter is wonderful. I want to take her to meet my friends and maybe come and sing at the El Mirador sometime. If she doesn't have any riding clothes, I'll take her and buy her some."

So, he took me to Marge Riley's place, which was downtown Palm Springs. Marge Riley was the western clothing designer who made all the clothes everybody wore in the desert. I still have the pink suede outfit Marge made me for the Desert Circus parade. Ray got me these Levi's, the boots and the whole dang thing and we went riding. We became the best of friends.

He was a dear dear friend and I guess I loved him.

THE MAYPOLE

Have you ever thought that you are the Maypole
That has all those lovely ribbons tied to the top?
With a hand at the end, attached to family or friend
Moving over and under, making patterns of wonder!
Somehow, as a Mother, You feel like that maypole,
With husband and children, fair weather friends
Weaving their problems around your skin
And while you stand there, tied so fast
Their hands let go and for air you gasp
Oh, could it be, that as Mother you have no other soul
But to play the role of your family's Maypole.

Roberta Linn

Wedding Bells

It was about this time I met my future husband, Freddie Bell.

I'll tell you where I met Freddie. I'm working at the Riverside hotel in Reno, which was owned by Mert Wortheimer. Now this is also part of the old Purple Gang, from someplace in the Midwest. That was the mob. He looked like a bulldog in the face, Mert not Freddie, but he was the sweetest guy and he used to sit and talk to me between the shows about all the mafia stuff.

I was working the main room and I was doing my Charlie O'Curran act, which I could still do today because it was that good. It had such great songs in it. There was an act in the lounge called Freddie Bell and the Bellboys. They were this rock and roll group out of Philadelphia. I used to go sit in the back and watch the Bellboys work, cause they didn't come on till after I finished two shows. I'd do a dinner show and a late show and then I'd go watch Freddie Bell and his group.

I thought, *this guy does great impressions*. He danced like Sammy Davis. He had the best looking band I'd ever seen in my life. All these guys were good looking Italian guys from south Philadelphia and they were just so well groomed. I thought they'd just stepped out of the band

83

box every time they came out and He (Freddie) was a looker too. He was really cute. And I kept looking at him and I thought, Wow, what a talent. He was funny. He could dance. He could sing and do impressions. He wasn't a great singer but he had style. They did rock and roll did standards and everything.

So, one night I come in late and I had on tennis shoes, Levi's and a turtle necked sweater. It was the winter and it was kind of cold up there in Reno. The reason I'm telling you this is because Freddie was maybe 5 foot 8 and I looked tall on stage with leotards cut up to my hip bones and high heels. So, I looked like I was six-feet tall on the stage.

I was standing at the back of the bar when someone comes up behind me and taps me on the shoulder. I turn around and it's Fred. He says, "Wow, you're not six feet tall! You wanna go to breakfast?"

I said, "What do you mean I'm not six feet tall?"

He said, "I've kind of been watching you work. I love the way you sing. I love your show. I love your legs. But, I was afraid you were too tall and I'd look like a midget next to you. Let's go have some breakfast when I finish."

That's how he and I met. We started writing material for each other. I started writing material for him. He started writing material for me, which I used again at the Moulin Rouge.

We just started dating and writing. He'd come to Vegas and I'd meet him there or go to Reno and back and forth in different places. Finally, he came to L.A. and asked me to marry him.

We had a whirlwind love affair. I just couldn't get enough of him. My mother had a fit when I went to Vegas the first time to meet him. She didn't like him. She said she was afraid he was going to ruin my career.

First Comes Love

Frank Sennis and Rocky Sennis didn't like Freddie Bell. They burned the midnight oil trying to talk me out of it, not wanting me to marry him - he's going to ruin my career, and so on and so on.

Fred and I had been dating back and forth from Vegas to LA to Reno to and finally, Fred came to my house in Los Angeles and asked my mother if it was OK if we got married.

My mother said, "No." She didn't like Fred.

He didn't much like her either. But, he put up with her for me.

She was really more concerned about my career. Because, her whole life she'd worked to help me have a wonderful career in show business. She'd made my clothes, paid my bills, played piano and taught me my songs. It was a big thing for my mother to lose me in her mind to somebody she didn't like.

However, he proposed and I accepted.

I already had a house in Vegas. We decided to get married at the little Church of the West. At that time, it was right next to the New Frontier. It had a little grassy knoll, a weeping willow tree, a steeple and it was really the little brown church of the west. It was really very nice and a lot of the Vegas entertainers have been married there over the years.

The ceremony was very funny and I have to tell you about my girlfriend. She was married to Johnny Drew. Her name was Jeannie Drew. If people have ever been to the Golden Nugget in Reno, they have this huge picture hanging over the bar of this beautiful redhead laying in the raw and that was Jeannie Drew. Johnny also owned the Riverside and was one of the owners of the Desert Inn.

Jeannie was quite a character and kind of liked to tip the bottle a bit. When I was getting ready to go to the little brown church of the west, she comes over and she's the one to take me. She arrives in this huge long stretch white limousine and we were to drive down Las Vegas Boulevard. This was before all the traffic there is now. She drove down it at about ninety miles an hour to the church and I had to close my eyes and pray. I didn't think I was going to be able to make it. I thought I was going to be dead.

But, we got to the church. The ceremony was fine. The Bellboys were all there looking their Italian finest, as if they could anything but. The minister had a lisp. My brother was our best man and I could see out of the corner of my eye, he was laughing so hard at this guy with this lisp that he was shaking all over. We got through the ceremony and then we went back to the Stardust hotel where we had a beautiful reception. I had a cake that if I were to put it on the floor it would reach the ceiling. That's how many tiers it had. It was gorgeous. All our friends and the band and all the entertainers on the strip came and thank goodness we did have that night off. We spent our honeymoon at my house, on Housel Street. I can remember Fred calling his mom and asking her how to make pasta fazull late that night when we got home.

We got married October 1, 1961 and we didn't really

get a honeymoon until January. We had an agent who booked us on the Cunard line to Hawaii. We had a working honeymoon.

We had never been on a ship before, either one of us. We had the white pants on with blue jackets with little crests on them. We did two shows going over, one show coming back and one show at the Royal Hawaiian in Hawaii and they gave us twenty three days of paid vacation. All the Bellboys came with us, because we had to have the band. In fact, even my conductor, who had been with me since I was just a kid, did all my arrangements came. His name was Billy Rose, like the Billy Rose from New York, and he brought his wife. The cruise, the hotel rooms, everything for all of us, was paid for. That was our honeymoon. I loved every minute of it. I learned how to drink Mai Tai's and we had a wonderful old time.

Then we returned home and went right back to work. Of course, I was still working the main rooms and Fred was still working the lounge. Then I discovered I was going to have little Freddie. So, I worked right up until, gosh I was doing the twist while I was pregnant at seven months at the Desert Inn and the Stardust. I often joked Freddie Jr. was going to come out looking like a corkscrew.

I had really planned to have the baby in Vegas. All my doctors were there. But, we, my mother and Fred and I, went to go see my Aunt Dean in South Gate, California and it happened. It was the Fourth of July holiday weekend and I was carrying a tray of dishes into the living room. I had open toe shoes and I caught my toe on a telephone cord and went down on my knees very hard. I didn't spill a drop on the tray, but I really banged myself up and while I was sitting on the couch next to my aunt maybe half an hour or forty minutes later, I said, "Gee Aunt Jean, I think I had an accident. I think I peed my pants."

She said, "What?"

I said, "Yeah. It's really bad."

"Oh my God," she said. "Roberta, I think your water is broken from the fall."

Sure enough it had. So, I did have a wonderful doctor I had been going to for years in Hollywood before I went to Vegas, Dr. Boris. He was my lady doctor, my Gynecologist. I talked to him and said, "You know I'm in trouble. I think I'm going to have my baby here instead of Vegas".

He said, "You better meet me at Cedars of Lebanon hospital right away." It's one of the best hospitals on the west coast.

Mom and Fred and I get in the car and we're on the freeway driving the wrong way, towards San Diego, and I said, "Hey you guys. I'm going to have this baby in the car. You're going the wrong way. You're going towards San Diego. We need to go in the other direction."

My mother said, "Aw, shut up and let us get you there." They were both nervous and I'm sitting there worrying about what's going to happen with the baby. Finally, they realized a few miles down the road it was the wrong way and they turned around and got me to the hospital.

Dr. Boris met us there and he said, "Oh honey. It's too soon. You shouldn't have this baby this soon. This baby's very small and it's too dangerous. You're going to have to bear with me. I'm not going to give you anything for the contractions once they start because it'll slow the baby down and could cause some serious problems."

So I said, "Well, whatever you tell me, I'll do." I had fifteen hours of really tough labor and there was only thing keeping me from really going nuts. Because, I was so naïve, I had no idea what was really going on. My mother and I never talked about sex; I never undressed in front of my mother ever, never. It was just our way, our Iowa family was very modest.

In the room with me was this lady from some foreign

country with a very distinct accent, and it was so funny as I look back. I think it was hilarious because she was mad at her husband. She was cussing him out all night and every time she was having a contraction she'd scream, "You son of a bits, you son of a bits, you'll never touch me again." Man, it was funny. The nurses were all laughing so hard. At the time, I didn't think it was funny, but as I look back at it, it was hilarious.

About fifteen hours into it, Dr. Boris decided the baby had to be born. I had a natural childbirth and I was completely worn out. It was a tough labor. The baby was only four pounds and eighteen inches long. My husbands' real name was Fernando Demonico Bello, but his professional name was Freddie Bell. So, my sons' real name is Fernando Dominico Bello, Jr.

But, when they put him in the incubator, I went over to look at him through the glass and the label on the crib said 'Bell Boy.' It had the last name and the sex and the United Press, the AP wire service and the other media sources came in and took pictures of it and the baby, running photos in their papers with the tag line "Roberta Linn gave birth to another Bell Boy." It was really cute.

By the way, Frank Sinatra sent a whole room full of flowers. He was crazy about Fred. You know, the whole Italian background, we all hung out together in Vegas. They all went to the gym and steam room together, Frank and Dean and the Rat Pack.

There's one other thing I think was important about this whole episode, and it was so cute, because the day I was able to bring Freddie Jr. home, the front page read, 'MARILYN MONROE FOUND DEAD.' I have this paper by the way, and on the inside, there's a picture of me taking the baby out of the hospital in a wheelchair. The papers ran this headline over my photo: 'ONE COMES IN AND ONE GOES OUT.'

After our baby was born, I was still doing my solo act in Vegas and on the road; places in New York, the Cork club and so on. Fred was still in Vegas, sometimes late at night, with his group. So, after our first baby was born I used to go over and get on stage with Fred. We'd mess around and sing some songs and rib each other. The twist was in at the time and I'd dance it with him. It was fun.

I was married and occasionally I still did other venues in other places. In fact, one time I was rehearsing Can-Can, my son, Freddie Jr. had a hundred and five fever. We thought we were going to lose him. And here I am trying to rehearse for the show. It was a big thing to work with Ricardo Montalban, him starring in the Pistache role.

Freddie's fever down, got him past it, but Rosioles, which he had, is an inside measles that suddenly breaks out on children and it's very dangerous. It can take a baby and he was just an little infant at the time. He was in the hospital's children ward down in San Diego at the time.

We did the Circle Arts theatre, a theatre in the round, and it was just a marvelous show. The measles was just the kick off to my involvement. During the show we did matinees and evening performances, so it was a very grueling pace.

Ricardo had been in a motorcycle accident prior to the show and he had a bad leg. He hid it beautifully and still does after all these years, smoothly getting on and off the stage. Theatre in the round, you can work pretty loose, but you have to be in the right places to cover your exits and costume changes. He did a beautiful job on that.

But, we were getting into these matinees and I had big songs to sing: "I Love Paris" and "Se Magnifique" and some other wonderful Cole Porter tunes. For an afternoon show, I woke up that day what with the baby being sick, getting him well and the stress of everything, I started get-

When Freddie and I were married the cake was taller than I am. We were called a "Hurricane of Entertainment" by the Hollywood Reporter. We were one hell of an act.

This picture of the marquee at the Sahara Hotel and Casino in Las Vegas was used by 20th Century Fox as an album cover for Freddie bell, Roberta Linn, and the Bellboys.

One of my last publicity photos as a single before marrying Freddie.

I always loved this picture of Freddie and me together.
Isn't it wonderful to be young and in Love?

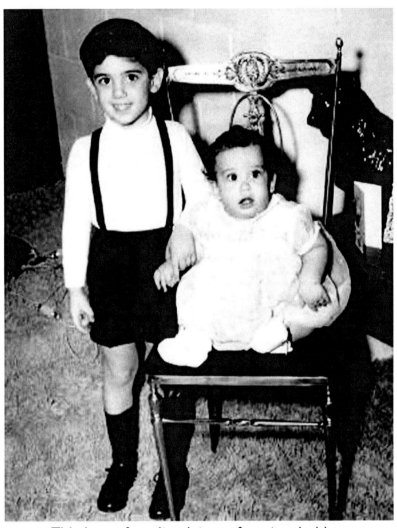

This is my favorite picture of my two babies:
Freddie Jr., and Angela.

Freddie Jr. on his prom night from Notre Dame High
School in Sherman Oaks, CA

Angela Bell was born April 16, 1966 in Las Vegas. Barbara Rickles, Don Rickles' wife, drove me to the hospital. These photos were taken as publicity shots. Angela performed in a Ragu commercial saying, "Mama Mia" after tasting the sauce and she performed alongside me at Sea World.

A late 1960's Vegas publicity photo. Fred hated me as a
blonde and made me change it right back.

97

ting a little sore throat. So, I remember my singing instructor used to tell me that if you mashed up onions, put them on a plate with some lemon juice and a little salt and pepper, made a liquid out of it and drank it; it would soothe the vocal chords. It would help.

Well, at the end of the first act, when I did "Se Magnifique" I was trying to seduce Ricardo Montalban to leave my dance hall open. So, I'm in a black negligee. I'm the merry widow with the long black stockings and the see through bodice and I sing my song to him while pushing him down on the chaise lounge. I was just literally jumping on him to give him a big kiss.

To make a long story short, I gad onions on my breath and when I gave him the kiss, his feet shot up in the air and when the lights turned out he smacked me on the behind. When I got home that night I still had his hand print on my rear. My husband said, "What is that on your butt?" and I told Freddie, "That was how Ricardo even with me for eating onions before the performance." The onions worked but I got a whack on the rear from Ricardo that lasted three days. I never ate onions again whenever I worked with anyone.

A New Act is Born

Stan Irwin, owner of the Sahara, caught us one night and said, "You know you guys are really good together," and then he added, "Have you thought of teaming up?"

I said, "I don't think I can. I'm still working for Frank and Rocky Sennis and I don't think I can do that."

"Well you know, "Irwin said, "Louis Prima and Keely Smith are leaving. They want to go to the Desert Inn. If that happens I want to give you a seven year contract. You can stay at home with your baby and enjoy your house, enjoy your husband, enjoy your life."

He was giving us this entire story and I thought, *seven years, forty something weeks a year in Vegas, good money and every year a raise.* Who could turn that down?

We became Roberta Linn, Freddie Bell and the Bell-boys at the Sahara. It worked out really really great for us and in 1966, Angela Madge Bello came around.

Frank and Rocky weren't happy. Number one, they burned the midnight oil with me. Freddie was pretty much a rounder. I was considered much of a lady. We're just as different as white snow and asphalt.

But, I think that's what intrigued me about Freddie. The fact that he was so different from anyone I'd ever known and I thought he was a great entertainer. I was just really impressed with him.

Freddie and I worked with Maurice Chevalier at the Americana hotel in Puerto Rico. One of our gigs out of Vegas was, over five years, going twice a year to Puerto Rico and one of my wonderful memories was working with Maurice Chevalier. What a guy. What an entertainer. What a gentleman. He was so inspiring.

Initially, he came out to see us work. He sat right in front of us and if I say so myself, Freddie and I had a great show. We did comedy. We did impressions. My husband was funny. He did Rock and Roll. I did big band and ballads and I'll never forget Maurice Chevalier giving us a standing ovation, saying how wonderful we were.

I got well acquainted with him those five years, one time, we were there. He asked me to walk on the beach with him and with his great accent, he would talk to me about his movies like Gigi, American in Paris, etc. I used to love to hear him sing, "Every leetle breeze seems to whis-peer Loueese," with his French accent. He was so wonder-ful. It was so relaxing. He would walk along the beach in his little hat and we'd just share stories. But, to receive a standing ovation, from such a magnificent star as Maurice Chevalier, was incredible, what a treat, what an honor.

In the seven years of the contract and our marriage, when it was good, it was very very good and when it was bad, it was horrid. I didn't realize how much booze Freddie put away and when he drank it changed his whole person-ality. When we were working in Vegas he'd drink snifters of Cognac. That was strong stuff. Then after work, on the way home, we'd stop off at a couple of different Italian restau-rants where all the entertainers ate. One was called the Continental and another was the Leaning Tower of Pisa. The Italian community in Vegas was very tight and everybody hangs out together. So, we'd go and grab a bite to eat and he'd order a bottle of wine. I'd be lucky if I had half a glass but with Fred if it was one bottle it'd be another. Then the mood swings. He'd get to a point where he would…he would hit me.

I said something to him in the car one night and the next thing I knew my glasses were flying. Then he'd claim, "Aw baby, I didn't mean it."

Then the next day, he'd start all over again. He'd sleep and then go out with the guys, either some of the Bellboys or Dean Martin or sometimes Frank Sinatra, and play golf early in the morning, drinking on the golf course, then beers and martinis when they finished. After, he'd come home and sleep for a couple of hours, I'd cook dinner where he'd drink water glasses full of wine. It never dawned on me. Finally, that evening back at work the Cognac's started again.

We separated one time and Vic Damone got us back together. It's kind of a weird thing. He invited us to one of his Bahai meetings. He offered, "Try to get Fred to attend a meeting or we'll come to the house." Here we were brought up Catholic and Vic talked Fred into coming to one of the meetings.

Bahai covers all religions. Bahai Lao was a prophet who was imprisoned because of his religious beliefs. He was from Persia and people that didn't follow the Muslim religion were crucified like Christ on the roads. When they found out he was teaching other than the Muslim religion he was thrown in jail and while there he wrote all these prophecies for forty two years. And, although I did not swing away from my religion, I thought some of the things he had to say were very good. It's a very love everybody type of belief. Also, they don't believe in drinking or drugs and it really helped Freddie. I've thanked Vic Damone many many times for saving my marriage.

During the 1970's I went with a Jackie O hairstyle.

At one point in my career, I did a solo tour of Asia and this is one of the ads that ran for me. This was the Dusi Thani Hotel in Bangkok, Thailand. Dusi Thani means "City of Heaven."

103

It really helped Freddie. He got off the booze for a while, our marriage improved and we got back together. We went to Puerto Rico to entertain and there were some Bahai's there that came over for home meetings. They call these firesides.

I thought; if I get Freddie out of Vegas…, and the children need us… and so on and so on, it would help patch things between us, make us whole. I negotiated a whole tour for us, but behind his back. We finished our contract in Puerto Rico then we went to Caesar's Palace and then we hit the road. We opened the Sahara's Tahoe. We were working twice a year at the Americana, which was owned by the Lowe's corporation.

The Inn Crowd at the Beach

In the early 1970's, we decided to take a vacation, we'd just worked Tahoe, and we rented a motor home. So, it was mom and my husband, and the kids. We were headed to San Diego and as we drove through Newport Beach, there was a place that I'd worked at before I met Fred, called the Jamaica Inn. It used to be where a lot of the acts would go, it was a great place to break in their acts before going to Vegas and getting reviewed. They had a band lead by Joe Castro. It was at Avocado and Pacific Coast Highway and it had a lovely restaurant plus some motel rooms.

Anyways, to make a long story short, we were driving down Coast Highway, the ocean route to San Diego, and I see the place with a FOR LEASE sign on it. I wrote the number down unbeknownst to my mother or my husband and I got on the phone. There was a man by the name of Warner. I don't know if he owned the property, was leasing it, or what and he lived in Corona Del Mar. So, I got on the phone with him and asked, "What's the deal?"

He said, "It'll be $1650 a month and a percentage."

I said, "What kind of percentage?" I don't even remember what we worked out, but in today's language, $1650 for that place would be $10,000. It was 7,500 square feet. It had a huge kitchen. So, I negotiated the deal and then talked to Fred, "We're gonna go to Newport. We'll rent our house and see if we can make a go of this thing."

We didn't have an awful lot of money. We had a lot of property, but not much cash in hand. So, we had to get in on a shoestring. We went in there and scrubbed the kitchen and the cooler on our hands and knees. I decorated the place absolutely gorgeous. It was just beautiful with a showroom, a lovely dining room that held about seventy five people, a nice stage and on top of that, we had the motel. So, we opened and it was called "Roberta Linn and Freddie Bell's Inn Place."

We opened with a bang. We had one of the finest chef's in the world, Rudolph Reitlon. It was said he was the chef for Adolf Hitler. He was working at one of the country clubs and we stole him away from there. We had a house band and brought Frank Amos in. He was our conductor who we stole from the Copa Cabana in New York and he put a band together of all these guys who are big stars today. One of them, Tom Rainier, is a piano player who works with Frankie Randall. He's one of the leading players. They were all top notch people.

Anyways, we opened to unbelievable business. Everybody came in, all the stars. They used to take their yachts down from Marina Del Rey and come to the club. One night on stage, we had Michelle Lee, Jack Jones and Buddy Marino. We had Keely Smith, Louis Bellson and the Stan Kenton Band. Once or twice a month, I'd book in the big bands while they were on their way from LA to Vegas or between some big date. They'd come in during the middle of the week when they needed some filler to pay for their travel. So, I could put them up in the hotel and we had the Count Basie, we had the Woodie Herman, Lionel Hampton, Sarah Vaughan, well... you name them, we had them. Plus, Fred and I would have our shows and we were also very popular at the time.

Then Fred started drinking again, very heavy, and when you own a restaurant or a nightclub, you don't work twenty four hours a day, you work twenty eight. I had two little children and a husband who was fighting, and losing to, alcoholism. And, he got very mean so finally I told him I couldn't take it any more. "That was it," I said, "I love you, but I don't like you."

There were other problems too. Because, he didn't take care of business that cost us some legal problems, we had to close the Inn. Then Freddie went his way and I went mine. We tore up about $500,000 worth of contracts. Because when we weren't working the place, we'd put somebody else in to cover like Anita O'Day or Buddy Greco or some major acts allowing Fred and I to go out and work.

We learned a lot of bad lessons. We had a bar manager who was stealing from us. A waiter was dropping meat from the window of the men's locker room window out the back and taking our best meat. You have to lock the doors and check everybody's pockets. It's a terrible business.

It was a horrible time in my life; the divorce, I had to reroute my whole act again to working as a single. It was very difficult.

Freddie and I had gone back and forth several times but I just couldn't face the arguments and the hitting anymore. He'd get mad and then he'd apologize, telling me he didn't mean it. But, all abusive relationships are like that." I'm sorry honey, I didn't mean it" only works so many times. I didn't realize, I thought maybe because I wasn't as hip and he was from South Philly and he was a Rock and Roller. I was a square and I was told as much by his band.

But that was it. Our great act and our marriage was over. No longer would I play the straight to his wildness. I really loved him and I knew I would miss working with him.

It ended when we were back in Vegas, it was over.

I just knew I didn't want anything to do with him anymore. I didn't want to have the arguments anymore.

As I've said, in Vegas we all hung out together. When I was there it was a very tight community for the entertainers. It was a very tight family. I knew Frank Sinatra quite well from those days. Freddie used to hang out with Frank and Dino at the Sands health club. Sinatra used to call my husband the Little Dago. Most people wouldn't dare say that unless they're Italian.

When Frank found out we weren't together anymore, I ran into him at the Trinidad restaurant here in Palm Springs, and he called me over to the table. You never Approached Frank's table unless he called you over, in case he was talking to someone or he was in a mood. Even though he might like you, he was kind of picky about that. So, he called me over and he said, "I hear you and the Little Dago are getting divorced."

I said, "Yeah, we are."

He blew up, "Is that guy crazy? You know you got two kids and everything."

I said, "Well, it didn't work out." I was a bit downtrodden on the whole thing.

Sinatra waved away the whole affair with his napkin and said, "I'm having a dinner party over at my house. I'll have my buddy Harry Guardino pick you up and bring you over."

I was really shy at the time. I wasn't the swinger type. I was quiet about and during my personal life. On stage I was a dynamo but in private I was very quiet and here comes Harry Guardino who was one of the clan. He picks me up and brings me over to Sinatra's house in Rancho Mirage, which he'd purchased from Spiro Agnew.

Frank was in the kitchen with his mother. She and Frank were in their making Linguini and Clams. They made a wonderful dinner. The dining room sat about twenty peo-

While at Sea World, I produced a TV special called Look Around the USA. During it I sang "Lovers in the Night and Strangers When We Wake" with the penguin on my left. During the rehearsals the real penguin, who I practiced with, pooped on me. So we went with the stand-in.

The most fun I ever had with a band in my life was when I had Roberta Linn and the Gamblers at Sea World. At first I didn't think I was country enough. But it didn't take me long to feel comfortable in a cowboy hat.

Champagne Lady

A Sea World publicity photo from the 1980's.

ple at these round tables. I sat next to Kirk Douglas and Burt Lancaster. I can remember the bar because Frank had just done the movie about Joey Lewis, the comic, called My Way, and he had this bronze head of Joe Lewis on the bar. It was one of his pride and joys. Then we went over to another building where he had his own private movie theatre which could have held thirty or fifty people. We sat on plush comfy couches and watched a Burt Lancaster movie.

It was a beautiful evening. Sinatra had wanted Freddie and I to get back together but if that wasn't going to happen then Frank wanted to see if Harry and I would work. Harry wasn't married at the time, but I was too square for him. I was also quite a bit younger than him and just not interested. The evening though was just a nice gathering of people in show business, doing it Frank's Way, and sharing in his hospitality.

The Rebirth

To reignite myself, I had to get all new arrangements. In fact, Frank Amos, who was my drummer, took some of my old arrangements and redid them for me because I didn't have any money. We'd lost our house in Vegas and had to file bankruptcy because of Freddie's friends and their bad advice. Divorce's are ugly and people don't think right.

So, now I'm with the kids and my mother and I'm trying to get started again. I went up to Sacramento to do a club and break in some material. We had the band with us and we had my coach, with all my music and the guy who was driving the truck said, "You know, there's something wrong here. All the stuff packed in the back is moving around. I want to change everything."

We went in to a diner to get something to eat while the driver pulled the cases out and some thieving kids drove around to the back of the truck and picked up the cases, stealing all my music. They were low riders and they must have thought they were going to get musical instruments. But instead they took all my music and there I was stranded again. No music in Sacramento.

I had to fake my way through the night I had hoped to break in a new act. I went on the radio pleading for my music back. I said, "They're not good to anybody without the lyrics. Please don't destroy them." We hung around up there for several days and the Sheriff's department found my music dumped in a river somewhere. It was all soaked through and through.

It was a very sad time. I just sat down and started to cry.

Finally, to try and get things going again, I moved back with my mom in the city of Downey, California and my brother Bill was helping me with the kids a bit. I started working again and picking up a few dates.

It was the late seventies and Vegas had changed. I was not a lounge act. I was a main room act, but I gave up that to work with Fred in the lounge at the Sahara. We eventually got away from that when we went to the Copa New York. We were the main room act, and at the Court club in Houston. Basically, because Fred and I didn't have a TV show, we didn't have a hit record and therefore together or solo we weren't able to swing'em a second time in Vegas. We were still very big names, but the fact that I had given up the Main room identity for him, made it very difficult.

I worked the Sahara Tahoe, I worked in Reno, New York, but it was tough. I had the kids. They were little and it was hard for me to get away.

I have to be honest. Some of the things that were distasteful to me, I've blocked out in my mind. I have to really stop and think about my life. People I don't like, I can't remember their name to save my soul. If there's someone I don't like, who's done something bad to me or my family, I just have a terrible time remembering their names. It's a defense mechanism I have, blocking these things out.

Eventually, I moved back to the San Fernando Valley and that's when I met this agent who put me in working with the Sound of Glenn Miller. That's when I went on the

Glenn Miller tour with the ModernAires, Bob Eberle and the Glenn Miller Orchestra. We worked out in Valencia at Magic Mountain. They had a big amphitheatre. It went over so well they held us over for two weeks. Then we left and went all up through Canada, and then down the west coast through Vancouver, Portland, and Seattle to San Francisco.

I had met a fellow who sang with the ModernAires and we kind of had a nice relationship. He was trying to help me with a few things. I worked down at the Smoke House on Venture Boulevard, amidst a lot of other little jazz clubs. That's where the Captain and Tenille played before they got their big record Love Will Keep Us Together and that's where I met my second husband, Jim Ferris, who was in the nightclub business. I went with him a couple of years and then we got married living in a house we bought in Reseda. But, the relationship with Jim didn't last either. We married September 16th, 1976 and were divorced a little more than a year later on January 11th, 1978

I was invited down to Sea World to do a show at their supper club by Cal Foster, who ran their entertainment, and he liked me so much he offered me a five year contract. I was thrilled. So, for a while I was commuting and I rented apartments for the band, I had regrouped my band from Vegas, and myself.

They had a beautiful supper club there called the Atlantis. I signed the contract and it was a blessing but it wasn't very much money. It wasn't the kind of money I made in Vegas but it was a five year contract. Something I could use to get the kids through school and help take care of my mom.

But, I still had the place in Reseda which I only spent two nights a week in because I was five days a week in my apartment in San Diego. Eventually, I sold the house in Reseda and we moved to San Diego. My son and daughter went and finished school there. I had a wonderful wonderful (wunnerful wunnerful) time at Sea World. It was probably one of the nicest times in my career and I filmed a TV Special there.

I was also able to take a tour of the Orient. I went to the Philippines and worked. I did an eight week tour and traveled to Jakarta, , Bangkok, Hong Kong and Tokyo all the while keeping my gig at Sea World.

I started out with the guys who worked with me in Vegas but they didn't want to stay so I hired a band from San Diego. For Milton Shed, who loved western music and was one of the founders of Sea World, I always included a bit of Country Western in my act, even though I did Jazz and Show Tunes. Urban Cowboy, with John Travolta, had just come out, everybody was wearing cowboy hats, boots and Milton said to me, "Have you ever thought of putting a country band together?"

I said, "Welp, No I haven't because I'm not sure I would be accepted. I'm not really a country singer."

He said, "Yes you are. You sing real good country. I'll tell you what. I'll put you on a retainer. You hire a band to come in and cover for you while you're out and I want you to go out and put together a country band. You name it and I'll buy it."

I went out to all the country joints wearing my Levi's and my boots, I was skinny at the time, and hired me seven of the most wonderful musicians, who were also the best looking guys you'd seen, and they could double on instruments while singing up a storm. I named the Roberta Linn and the Gamblers.

I let my hair grow down to my waist. I wore Indian headbands. We did Patsy Cline. We did Rock-a-Billy. These guys were excellent. I don't know who was better than the other. They could even do on spot harmony. There was no music in front of us. We rehearsed two or three days a week during the afternoons at the Atlantis and people would come in and listen. That show took off like, you guessed it, Busters Gang. The country stations loved it.

We got so popular, the people were five and six abreast all the way out into the parking lot waiting for seats. You couldn't get in the place and we did three shows a night. It was just unbelievable. The Gamblers and I opened for Alabama when they came into San Diego and I had us all set to go National to record and a couple of the guys began to think they wanted to start their own group. Egos took over, the group broke up and I had to put another band together.

This time I changed the whole theme. I called them the Big Apple. We did Count Basie and all the big band swing. The guys wore tuxedos, slicked their hair back and donned carnations. It was a nice thing but I loved that country band. It was one of the favorite times in my life. I think if I could have kept them together I would have stayed Roberta Linn and the Gamblers, I've got some great memories of that.

Eventually, the guys who started Sea World lost the place and then Anheuser Busch took over. When this happened, Cal was on his way out and Mr. Shed was gone. It just wasn't the same anymore. It was the late Eighties and I started going on the road again, which I hated.

It was difficult again. I felt like I'd restarted my career for the umpteenth time. I did a couple of cruises, Sitmar Lines. I was kind of spoiled now because I'd gotten to settle down, but I was forced to travel again and then my mother got very sick.

I needed to stay rooted. I was offered a job by the Lowes Corporation, which I had worked for in Puerto Rico as entertainment director, to sing for them at their new resort opening in Scottsdale, Arizona. I got that when I called Bill Maiback, who was Bob Tisches right hand man, I saw they were opening the resort, and I called him and said, "I'm looking for something. My contract has run out at Sea World and I would like job."

He said, "Why don't you come over and see me."

I went and got the job. When I first started there Momma went with me and got sick. She had a heart attack while I was having lunch with her. I got her home to San Diego. But, I was having troubles with my daughter then too. She was having serious problems with drugs and running away. But, it wasn't too long before I got things as in order as I could and I returned to Scottsdale to make some money.

I was flying back and forth to see my mother at the house in San Diego. One day I got a call from my girlfriend who had ten children. Her oldest daughter was staying at my place watching over my mother for me. She called and said, "You'd better get back to San Diego. You're mother has been rushed to Intensive Care."

So, I went back and my girlfriend, Lolita Kohler, who's one of my dearest friends and lives in Phoenix, she said, "Maybe I should go with you."

My mother was in Mercy Hospital in San Diego. It's hard for me talk about this. We went up and saw my Mom. We visited all afternoon. She looked really good. She had on her slippers and robe and sat on this chair, we talked for hours and then I went to dinner with my girlfriend and family. While we were gone she'd had a code blue. For three days they had her on the respirator and everything. I'd slept on the floor. But then they called us at dinner and said she wasn't going to recover.

Besides being my mom, she'd been deeply involved with the evolution of my career, my clothes, and my whole style. She was my best buddy, my friend and mother.

That was a tough time. I went in for a deep funk, a depression. My girlfriend, her mother and her son stayed

Elizabeth and Alex Kasza Kasser with Zsa Zsa Gabor
and myself attending a party for Zsa Zsa's mother
Jolie Gabor at Le Vallauris in Palm Springs.

Actor Greg Juarez
hosted a party for
me when I got my
star on the Palm
Springs Walk of
Fame. He always
hosted the best
parties.

with me for a time. I quit working for while. I just couldn't do anything. I ended up working for some small clubs around San Diego.

A Timeshare Boot Strap

A very dear friend of mine, Henry Maxwell, who lived in San Diego, had taken over a place called the Desert Isle, timeshare, on Highway 111 in Palm Springs. He'd seen me sing at some clubs and he said to me, "Why don't you come over and stay a couple days with us over here, take a look at the resort and maybe you could help us with entertainment. Besides, this would give you a little break from San Diego."

My son was still at home then, and thanks to Henry I got started in timeshare. He had some guy doing the podium he was unhappy with and he grabbed me by the hand. I knew nothing about timeshare. I went in the podium room. There was a television and they had somebody on the film for RCI, that's Resort Condominiums International, and Henry said, "Now see that. All you have to do is show them the film and be nice to the people. That's all you have to do. You can do some entertainment, you get own office, a nice salary and you can get yourself together again." So I did that for a while.

During the time I was there I was asked to be Desert Circus Queen again. We did a kind of déjà vu the desert scene called the Desert Circus, which was a revisit of an older theme which was once upon a time the biggest event in the desert. Trini Lopez was the Grand Marshall and I was the Queen. It was a lot of fun.

In the meantime, I had to pay my bills. I didn't go into therapy, but I needed some time. I took on the distributor for singing machines, Karaoke. I was one of the first distributors in California. They were put out by a company called Singing Machines. I thought, these are kind of fun. So, I sold the machines on the side.

Eventually, because I was not making enough money to take care of the kids and my home while I was gone, I was trying to find my way out of this whole I'd dug myself into and it was getting deeper.

I rented the house, while I was working for Desert isle. My house in San Diego was a mess. Four young attorneys rented it and they just thrashed it. Now, I've got to get back in there to save the house and I gave up the thing at Desert Isle.

While I was in my funk, I got into a car wreck. I was so depressed I finally began selling off my personal treasures. The handwriting was on the wall and I wanted to save my house and I was on my rear end financially, struggling, not wanting people to know I was having such a hard time. I was working little joints here and there and barely existing. It was enough and I was trying to make it work. I sold my autograph book to raise the money to pay my mortgage. It was a fantastic book. A little girls signature collection book, all autographed to me. It was about six inched long and four inches wide and full of memories. I'd had it from all those years in Hollywood. People I'd actually worked with had signed it; Anna Mae Wong and Shirley Temple, Cary Grant, Clark Gable, Jimmy Durante, you name it they were in my book. I saw an advertisement for a fella who wanted Hollywood memorabilia and I went to see him. I even sold one of my husbands 1950's old guitars. I did everything I could to save my house. I even sold some jewelry. I hated doing it and still regret it, but I made it.

I finally found a strategy with some success. How I survived was by renting the bedrooms to some of the foreign college students out of La Jolla. My house was situated in a very nice area. I had a big den, a formal living room, six bedrooms and three and a half baths on a cul-de-sac, so it was an ideal location, close to everything. I rented out the big rooms, two or three at a time and got maybe fifteen hundred a month from the students. I had them from all over the world. One batch of them was from Switzerland, another single guy was from Venezuela. Then there were two little girls who were much too rich for their own good from Japan. It was a time for survival. They came in and I survived.

Things were getting better but I still couldn't see the light at the end of the tunnel. I didn't know what to do and my girlfriend, whose daughter was going for her Real Estate license, suggested I do the same while recovering from my accident.

Together, we went to Anthony's Real Estate school and I sat in the back of the room looking terrible. I passed my test and never thought I was going to use it.

Then some people who worked for Lawrence Welk timeshare came over because they were looking at buying Desert Isle. They saw me and said, "What are you doing here? You should be working for Lawrence Welk." They asked me to talk to them and I did and I started doing dinner parties for Lawrence Welk timeshare in Escondido, California. Their Marketing Director liked me and hired me.

I hosted my first solo Dinner party at the Embassy Suites over near Anaheim. First of all, we'd run an ad in the paper so we could hire the people I wanted to work with me. Now, I'm commuting from San Diego to all these places, the Welk organization sent me, in my little van because I wasn't working at the resort. I was working for the

Marketing department. These places were all over the place; Anaheim, out in L.A. by the airport, they could be anywhere within driving distance. It was a big job riding around. Sometimes I'd sleep with my brother's place in Downey.

The dinner parties were wonderful. I'd have maybe 250 guests. I'd have twenty to thirty young people, nifty looking kids with a lot of personality. There'd be maybe three couples to a table with one of my representatives. During my presentation, I'd talk about my days with Welk, working the ballrooms, and Lawrence Welk with his funny little accent telling people to "Pee on your clothes" when he meant "Be on your toes," a light airy fun kind of thing telling them about the resort. Each of the reps would get a fifty dollar deposit from a guest wanting to attend the full presentation. I had a nice gal working for me, Gloria, who would take the deposits and write out their slips. Then the people would go to the resort, take a tour and they'd buy. We were selling, I've been told, as high as 60-67 per cent off of those tours at the Lawrence Welk resort in Escondido.

This was my really big step into the timeshare industry. When the fellow that was doing the marketing was fired by Lawrence Welk, Jr., I found myself back on the road again singing. But, that didn't stick. It felt like I'd backtracked further down the tunnel because none of the gigs were big enough. While shopping in San Diego I ran into some of the people I knew from the Lawrence Welk resort and they asked, "What are you doing?"

I answered, "Oh, I'm living out of a suitcase. I'm out on the road trying to make a living."

Then John, said, "We're working for Winners Circle resorts under Jim Watkins, at the Gas Lamp Plaza suites downtown San Diego."

I was aghast, "Downtown San Diego. Who wants to

live or work down there?"

He said, "Wait. It's going to be the coming place. It's a great little resort and they need a speaker. They'll give you a base pay of a thousand dollars a week plus a percentage of the sales."

I said, "That sounds like a pretty good deal," and thought, It's not what I'm used to making but it's at least a way to go.

I got the job at the timeshare in the Gas lamp district of downtown San Diego while I was renting rooms to the exchange students, but I'd never done any direct sales. I'd only been the speaker and hosted the marketing dinners. But they had so many people attending they were turning people away and giving people presents. I went to Jim Watkins and said, "Hey, I got an idea. I know enough about this. Why don't I do the front end for the sales people and pick out the ones most interested and as the sales people become available we'll turn the customers over to them. I'll be their sizzle. Then the sales people will only have to do the back end of the sale."

Jim said, "Let's try it and see how it works."

Well, it saved them thousands and thousands of dollars in gifts that were being given to people they were turning away and we were making thousands and thousands of dollars in sales. So finally Jim said, "Since you're doing so well, at least on the last tour of the day, pick a couple you like the best and try a sale."

So, I was now podium, sizzle and sales person. We sold out the Gas Lamp Plaza suites and Jim decides to buy a place up by Disneyland called Dolphins cove, which was a HUD property. He ran all these poor Mexicans out of it, some of whom were still living in the back.

He developed the front end of the place. We're booking tours and selling on the premise of a year down the line. I tell you, the Mexicans were marching out front with signs, angry because we'd moved them out. It was the biggest mess I'd seen in my life. We were trying to dress up the place. We were working to put together a beautiful speaking room with a lot of my pictures with celebrities, and my trophies and stuff. We were putting out food for the tours to eat as they came in. The food was out there and the cock roaches are crawling over the food while we're trying to sell and I finally said, "Jim, I've got to get out of here. I can't do this."

In the meantime, I was living in a motel next door and commuting to San Diego again. Still hanging on to my house by the tips of my fingers and toenails and now I didn't know what I'm going to do. I didn't have a job and I didn't want to go back on the road again.

Then, someone I worked with a Dolphin's Cove said, "You know Marriott is going to open up a resort in Newport Beach. They don't do speakers but with your experience and the time that you've had, you know, who knows?"

My Life with Marriott

I set up an appointment with Rick Owens and Russell Aberathny at the Marriott hotel in Newport Beach and I pestered these people and pestered them. I said, "I need this job. I want this job. I know I can do a good job for you." They hired me along with four other people and they called us the Dream Team.

There wasn't a shovel in the ground yet and we started to sell. There was a big white tent and I was on the road again because, with this Dream Team. We did our own marketing; we went out to the convention centers, set up a booth, got our own leads and booked our own tours. Sometimes I'd bring home five or six hundred leads and then a girl would type up a letter if I hadn't already booked them to come into the hotel for the presentation. All we had was pictures, a white tent and a beautiful view of the ocean. This is how we started Newport Coast for Marriott.

We were called the Dream team and we truly were the Dream Team. We did five jobs. We went out to give the presentations, we booked the people, we sent out the invitations and letters, we followed up with a phone call, set the date and then we toured them. Five of us did all this.

Out of the first year, although I didn't do a whole year there because I wanted to move back out to Palm

Springs and be with my friends, family and son, I did close to a million dollars in sales from only April till the end of the year.

That's how I got with Marriott. We did Marketing and Sales. It was really a big job. I was very tired. It was one of the reasons I wanted to come out to Desert Springs. I'd heard wonderful things about it from the owners I'd met and toured in Newport Beach. I sold my house in San Diego, just at the right time. I was able to take some money out of that and put it into the stock market in the late 1990's. Luckily, I got out at the right time too.

I worked at Newport until I transferred over to Desert Springs, in Palm Desert, and worked for Sue Sanders, where I did the In-House, doing direct marketing and sales. My first year back in the desert, I was Sales Person of the Year and I still work for Marriott today, six years later.

Palm Springs is my home and I don't think it will ever see a downturn again, with all the building we're seeing here, the industry coming in, tourism, and casinos, Palm Springs has reached a peak and we're going to continue to see it grow. My prediction is that in the next four or five years, Palm Canyon Drive will be endless hotels and motels and restaurants. Some people think it is already.

That's where I'm at today. I'm comfortable in my home. I've been with Marriott now for my sixth year.

In the future I'll continue to work. I would like to do another album. Perhaps, all original songs, I've written a lot of songs and maybe do some of my earlier songs or maybe both. I could do a Jazz album of my Uncles songs and call it All in the Family, songs like Boulevard of Broken Dreams, Lullaby of Broadway, September in the Rain, I'll String Along with You, I Only Have Eyes for You. He wrote some magnificent songs. To me, that would be what I would like to do as a final comeback. I will continue working as long as I can and that's about it.

The Murder of My Friend

I know I mentioned some of this earlier in the book, but if you'll bear with me a couple of paragraphs you'll see the importance of why I want to repeat myself just a little.

I came into Palm Springs for the first time back in the early 1950's. I was on television and quite well known at the time from the Welk show and I had been invited down to sing at the Tennis club, on Baristo, at a $100 a plate cancer dinner for Cobina Wright. It was a lot of money in those days. Today it would be a $1000 or $2000.

At the end of the evening, after I had sung, and everybody who was anybody in Palm Springs was there, this very handsome man came up to me, in his tuxedo and said, "I just love the way you sing. I'm having a party at my hotel tonight, the El Mirador hotel, and I'd love for you to be my guest."

I didn't realize who I was talking to. It was Mr. Ray Ryan, who owned the El Mirador hotel, and he was a very famous guy. He was part of the very high social set in Palm Springs. He was an oilman from Texas, which I didn't know at the time, and a partner of H. L. Hunt out of Dallas, Texas, who was one of the richest men in the world. His kids, the Hunt brothers cornered the market on silver in the 1980's and I guess they own a couple of big ball teams and so on.

129

I was very flattered to have this gentleman talk to me and it was quite a party I was already attending at the Tennis club. The old Tennis club was the place to go at that time. It's now a timeshare.

Anyways, to make a long story short, my mother was with me and she was very very protective of me. I was quite young then, 18 years old. She decided we were not going to the party at the El Mirador.

In the meantime, we had been put up in a motel, which was very nice. There were lots of nice little boutique hotels in that area. I believe most of them are still operating. Palm Springs seems to have gone into a renaissance craze over that style of architecture.

The next morning at about 8 o'clock, I hear a car horn outside. A kind of do-do-da-do and I thought, 'What the heck?' and there's a big loud knock on the door. There standing was this gentleman who was in his tuxedo the night before only now he's wearing his boots, Levi's and a ten gallon hat. He had one of those cute little Ford Thunderbird's with two big long white horns on the front it. He was quite an outgoing kind of guy and he says, "Miss Roberta Linn? How come you didn't come to my party last night?"

And I said, "Well, it was kind of late and my mother said we shouldn't go."

Then he said, "Well, you missed a nice party. I'm sorry you didn't make it. But, I'd like to take you horseback riding."

I said, "What's your name again?"

"Ryan. Ray Ryan."

"I don't have any clothes to wear for horseback riding."

And he said, "I'll buy you some."

So, I looked at my mom and asked, "Mom, would you mind if I went horseback riding?" Which I loved to do and I was a pretty good horseback rider and so was my mom.

She said, "It's OK, if you'd like to go, but what about clothes?"

"Mr. Ryan said he'd buy me some."

So, he took me to Marge Riley and she was the lady who outfitted everybody in western clothes. At the time, Palm Springs was very western. People wore western clothes, boots and hats everywhere. There were the Desert Riders that had horses and lots of people were members. They conducted moonlight rides and morning breakfasts with Tex Kidwell who was kind of the Troubadour of the group and would set up the campsites ahead, making sure eggs and bacon and beans were all prepared upon our arrival. Everybody who was anybody went on rides.

Ray took me and bought me some very expensive Levis and boots and off we went riding. And that was the beginning of a very very deep friendship with Mr. Ryan. We'd leave from Smoke tree stables, where they kept the horses, and we'd ride and ride and ride out across the desert. From that time forward, I used to come down and go riding with Ray whenever he was in town.

He did a lot of world traveling even to Saudi Arabia. He told me he went over there to make deals for his oil interests with H.L. Hunt.

Then whenever he was in town, I'd come over to the El Mirador and we'd see everybody there from Dean Martin to Jimmy Durante to Errol Flynn, you name it. All the stars stayed at the hotel and there were some marvelous parties.

Frank Bogert, who later became Mayor of Palm Springs, was managing the hotel for Ray. Frank was a real cowboy. We used to go out on these beautiful rides. I remember this one night going out with the Desert Riders, Frank and Ray and in the dark we could hear these two English accents talking and laughing and making all kinds of an uproar. When we got off our horses I realized I was riding with Cary Grant and David Niven. I can remember looking at Cary Grant. Everyone else was a little dusty and wrinkled but when he got off his horse Cary Grant didn't have a wrinkle on him nor a speck of dust. I looked at him and said, "You know you really are perfect, aren't you" and he laughed.

The Desert Riders, I think they are still around, participated in the Desert Circus. Every year the city of Palm Springs would have an annual special event called the Desert Circus. I was, I think Mr. Ryan arranged this, Desert Circus Queen in the 1955. Kirk Douglas was the Grand Marshall.

I'll never forget this. I was riding on this Polo pony of Frank Bogerts' during the parade, and I had on these brand new boots and this beautiful outfit Marge Riley made special for me that was pink leather. It had a blue satin blouse with little butterflies on it and a cute little pink western hat with butterflies also. But, every time the drums would sound from the Marine band, Frank's horse would jump straight up in the air. I had blisters on my feet from the boots that were killing me too.

We made it through the parade and then we had the big rodeo, where Frank Bogert was the head guy. They had me at the gate, waiting to come out, and remember I was the Queen of the Desert Circus, the bleachers are filled and Frank announces me from his horse down in the arena, "Here she is, the Queen of Desert Circus, Miss Roberta Linn."

I couldn't get the horse to go through the gate. I did everything. I switched him with the reins. I kicked him in the sides. He wasn't about to move. So, Frank sees my dilemma and says, "Miss Linn will make her entrance in a minute. Here comes the Desert Riders." Out came about twenty kids on these little Quarter horses, hell bent for election, through the gate. All the sudden my Polo pony decides to take off with them. He heads straight for the other side of the arena and turns, because Polo ponies can turn on one foot I think. He makes a turn; the horse goes thisaway and I went thataway. The next thing I know I'm hanging under the belly of this pony, who is running like hell with my leg through the stirrup and I could've been hurt really bad. Frank Bogert rushes to save me and comes riding up on his horse, grabs me by the seat of my pants, lifts me onto my saddle and then says to the crowd, "Well, here she is folks, the Desert Circus Queen, Miss Roberta Linn."

I was so embarrassed. First of all, I had to take my boots off. I was riding in moccasins so I didn't have my heel against the stirrup, like I should have. But that was my grand entrance at the rodeo.

Over the years, I spent a lot of time coming back and forth from doing my TV show whenever Ray would come in town. I was really very smitten with him. I guess he was my first great love. He was twenty-six years older than I was and a great looking man. I had a real crush on him. He was the guy who was Catholic and married and had a very strange life. His wife was at the estate in Evansville in Indiana. There was a lot of money involved. I think everyone who came down from Hollywood stayed at Ray's El Mirador hotel. He was a lot of fun. He was a great guy.

He'd call me from all over the world. I can remember him calling me from Paris. It was about three or four o'clock in the morning and asking me to sing his favorite song. It was Melancholy Baby, which there'd been a lot of jokes about Melancholy Baby with the drunk in the back of the room shouting "Shing me Melon collie baby." But, it's a really beautiful song, with a lovely verse, and I'd be on the phone singing it to Ray while he was all over the world.

I did travel with him quite a bit too. We went to Cuba just before Castro took over. On the way we stopped off in

New Orleans. He was always meeting with some very important people. I had no idea. I was so young. I was so naïve. I had no idea who he really was or how important he was.

Cuba was absolutely fantastic. We stayed at the Intercontinental Hotel. George Raft was there and a lot of the big important people in the gambling industry. I don't remember all of their names, but I do remember they were very important people from all over the United States; Chicago, New York, Florida, Mob people, we're talking Mob people. And of course, George Raft was very much connected with them.

I remember we drove down to where Hemingway had his place where he did his writing down on the beach. The beaches were absolutely gorgeous and there was this big wall surrounding Havana, where the ocean would crash against it protecting perfume shops with interesting and fine-looking little perfume bottles. I still have some. They were made of real crystal and very expensive. Ray would buy them for me, these huge bottles of Joy and others. I can remember going to Harry's or something like that with this marvelous black man playing music and the gambling casinos with marble mosaic tile pools and this magnificent night club in the midst of a palm grove. I've never seen anything like it since and don't think I ever will again. The stage opened up like a flower, an orchid, and the show girls came out and danced on the petals and the band was there. I think the singing star was Ginny Simms. I have never seen a stage like that. I've never seen a presentation like that in my life. It was in a palm grove.

From then on, I never dated anyone else for six years and I would wait for Ray to come back to Palm Springs so I could visit him.

We used to go out to breakfast at the restaurant in the Bermuda Dunes airport. We used to ride all the way out there and hook up our horses. It was about a fifteen mile ride. There was nothing between Palm Springs and Bermuda Dunes at the time. Ray and his friend Ernie Dunlevie built Bermuda Dunes. It's now covered in nice houses. We also used to ride out to Indian Wells to Lucy and Desi Arnaz's hotel. But, Palm Springs was really the place for celebrities. There was Charlie Farrell's Racquet Club where you'd see Esther Williams, and every other big star in Hollywood and they all ended up at the El Mirador hotel.

Ray loved my singing. He told everybody about me and helped me put together my first show at Vegas. He got Charlie O'Curran to stage my act. Then, Charlies got Nelson Riddle to do my music and Edith Head to do my gowns. My very first singing date in Vegas, Ray Ryan actually put it together for me. I opened at the New Frontier with Marge and Gower Champion and received fantastic reviews.

From there, because of Charlie's connections, I worked at the Copacabana in New York. I also worked at the Shamrock hotel in Houston, which was owned by a friend of Rays, McCarthy was his name. He was an oilman. Their connections helped me get other connections and I did clubs all over the United States.

I can remember meeting Mr. McCarthy in New York. He had a girlfriend who was also a singer, April Stevens. Ray and I met him at his hotel and were talking to him for a couple of hours. He and Ray were talking about the oil business. I was just kind of sitting and listening, and then all of a sudden Mr. McCarthy says, "I have a friend here," she, April Stevens, was in the bathroom for two hours while they were talking because he was married and he didn't want anyone to know of his association with her. I'd known April for years and had no idea she was in the other room.

Another time, Ray came back from Saudi Arabia, while I was working at the Copa and he called me and said, "I have tickets for My Fair Lady. I'll be flying all night but the tickets are front row center and we shouldn't miss it. I'll pick you up." So, he sent me to this famous designer store in New York and told me to pick something out. I got this absolutely fabulous dress, it's one of my favorites, with a red velvet hat with roses all around the top and I wore my hair up. Julie Andrews was the star, and poor Ray, he fell asleep in the front row and started to snore.

During the time Ray was back, H. L. Hunt came in and rented the whole top floor of the Waldorf Astoria. So, after I closed at the Copa, we went out with H.L. and I had no idea at the time, but they were betting two to three thousand dollars a game on football. Mr. Hunt had a man who worked for him, a Mr. Venrables, who was his man who ordered everything for him, took all his phone calls and so forth. Mr. Venerables and I were watching television when all of the sudden Ray asked me, "Have you ever had caviar?"

I said, "No, I've never eaten caviar in my life."

He said, "Well, you're gonna try it today."

Ray and H.L. ordered this caviar. There must have been a mound of about twelve inches long and six inches high with all the condiments and stuck in ice next to it was a frosted bottle of Russian Vodka. Ray said, "Now, I know you don't drink a lot. But if you want to have some just sip it, because it's strong." I never had anything so good in my life. I'm sitting there while they're gambling, and watching television with Mr. Venerables, eating caviar and sipping Russian Vodka in the whole top floor of the Waldorf Astoria.

I don't know whether it was that day or a few days later but the ball team they owned was in town and Ray and H.L. had a boxed seat. It was so funny, because Mr. Hunt says, "We're going to see the ball game," to me and

I say, "That's fine." Here's this very wealthy man, who to me looks like Alfred Hitchcock. He ordered his limousine downstairs and he likes tuna fish sandwiches. So, he's got his little brown bag with a tuna fish sandwich in it while we're riding in this limo and we go the game. I'm sitting in there with Ray, H.L. and Mr. Venreables and this is the game where a player named Larson pitches a no-hitter. This was typical of my time in New York with Ray.

We also traveled to New Orleans a lot. He had a lot of business there and we'd stay at the Roosevelt hotel. There was a lot of gambling behind the scenes. Ray was one of the finest Gin players in the world and he loved to play there. There was also gambling all over Palm Springs at the time. I was never in on any of the big gambling things myself, but I was brought along.

Another time, we went to Baden, Germany together and I opened at the Harrah's club. All of this was planned by Charlie O'Curran, even though I was under contract from William Morris at the time, Charlie was very influential. I headlined at Harrah's. In fact, Louis Prima and Keely were in the Lounge. I was the headliner in the main room.

I worked the Sands hotel in Vegas with Danny Thomas. I was supposed to have gone in with Dean Martin and Jerry Lewis and done a movie. That's back when I got my first case of pneumonia so instead I ended up with Danny Thomas. He was really something.

At the same time, Ray was playing in one of his big Gin games where they'd play for three or four days at a time. They'd take a break in the bath and take an upper or coffee or something and then go back and play. There was always lots of money on the table. He felt I was good luck for him, so I'd sit with him sometimes and watch him play. I didn't realize the importance of what was going on there. I don't know much about cards. It seems to me he was one of the great players and people liked to play with him because he had a lot of money. Joe Bernstein, they called him the Silver Fox, was one of Ray's friends who was also a big time gambler. He was around a lot and Ray would sponsor him.

I didn't see Ray for a while and something had happened. He came and he was staying at the Desert Inn hotel and for some reason in a game, where he had played with I think it was Nick the Greek, or someone like that, some of the fellows from Chicago said he had cheated on the game and they were trying to extort money from Ray. So, he called me and told me that I shouldn't be around him because he was having some problems with people and it could be very bad for me. I don't think even then I understood the seriousness of what was going on. So, now he's got these people trying to extort money from him.

The man he was with turned him into the FBI and from that day on Ray's life was not the same for seventeen years. There was a hit ordered on him since one of the men who were against Ray was sent to jail. Then, in 1976 or 77, Ray and a friend were blown up in his car. They were at the Evansville Health club for men.

I was still in touch with him until then. We were still talking and everything but he was worried about my well-being. So, someone called mom and said, "Have you seen the paper today?" I said, "No. Why?" and they said, "Ray Ryan was blown up in his brand new Lincoln Continental with his chauffeur in Evansville, Indiana. There was a wire on it and it was such a big blast it blew windows out of apartment houses three blocks away.

But, that was the end.

I didn't come back to Palm Springs very much after that. The El Mirador hotel was sold and turned into the Desert Hospital. It was totally torn down except for the tower. It was during the time Ray was in hiding that the hotel was originally sold. I think Mr. and Mrs. Conti, a

On my first date with Ray, when he took me horseback
riding, he wore a cowboy hat like this one.

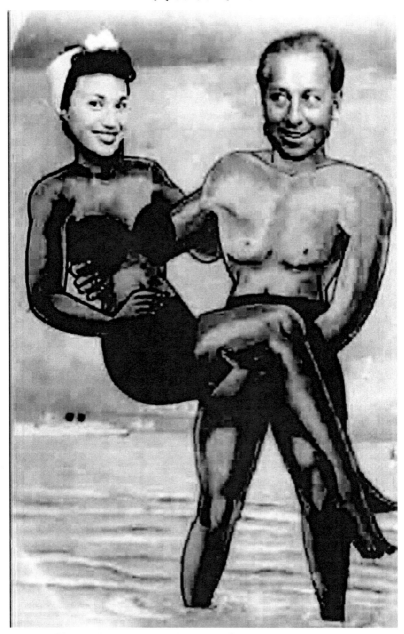

This photo was taken on Santa Monica pier.
Ray and I had good times together.

Ray Ryan owned the famous El Mirador Hotel up until his death. It was the number one celebrity hang out in Palm Springs. Here he is at breafkfast with Dean Martin and his wife Jeanne.

Over the years, I did a lot of fundraisers. I considered it a part of my responsibility of being a good citizen. My name is on the top center of this poster being held up by Frank Sinatra.

wealthy couple from Palm Springs, and a Mr. Fitzgerald, a friend of Ray's, had something to do with it and they eventually sold it.

When I did come back I sang at the Chi Chi club on Palm Canyon Drive on the northern end of town. It was a beautiful club. The motif of the place was the beach. Everybody worked there; Liberace worked there, Sammy Davis worked there, I worked there and my opening act was Dan Rowan and Dick Martin

But, after Ray was killed, and of course by this time I was married to my second husband Jim, I just didn't have the heart to come back. I did a few things at the Riviera hotel but Palm Springs just wasn't the same to me after Ray was gone.

The Last Chapter

I sang at the last show at the Sands hotel before it was blown up. It was an art deco theme with the whole ballroom decorated black and white and everybody wore black and white. It was filed with all the guests who had been frequented the Sands for years. Entertainers for many decades were to perform and I was a Guest Star. It was a New Year's Eve and shortly thereafter it was exploded on television and then replaced by the Venetian hotel and casino.

The show was wonderful and there was so many people on the strip that night it was like a lion roaring when midnight came around. You couldn't even drive down the strip. The city had closed the main road to all but pedestrian traffic. Like I said, it was New Year's Eve and at twelve o'-clock I was on the stage with the band and the other entertainers. They shot off cannons, pirates came out, the volcanoes went off, fireworks, and the people on the street erupted in applause and screams. It was unbelievable. You could hear it through the walls of the convention center at the Sands. It was the last show before they blew up the old Sands hotel and it couldn't have been on a more exciting night

We did a lot of nostalgia. Sang some of the songs

I'd sang with Danny Thomas. I did a medley of my Uncle's songs from the great musicals, things that pertained to the old days of Vegas. It was a lot of fun.

Over the last five or seven years, I've also continued to help some of my local organizations. I did a show for the Cathedral City Chamber of Commerce for a Mr. Settler, who is now the Mayor, at Rancho Mirage Country Club and we raised funds for the Senior Center and the Parks. They had these huge huge posters of me all over town and bill-boards too. That was a pleasure. I've always liked to do a lot of charity events.

I also did a fundraiser for Shelter for the Storm at the Westin hotel. I wrote a song for them called "Shelter from the Storm" that I recorded with the local Baptist choir, the Victory Singers, from the Victory Baptist church in Indio. The event was to raise funds for abused mothers and their children. We had a big band and an auction. They even auctioned off a miniature horse.

I produced a fundraiser for the Salvation Army and the Red Cross to raise money for the earthquake victims in both Northridge and San Francisco. These were just a few of the special things I've done recently.

There was also a night with Buddy Ebsen, Jane Wyman, Alice Faye and Keely Smith. They had a big band again and it was at Palm Springs High School. It was pro-duced by Terry Hill and Associates. It was a nice tribute to the stars. Buddy Ebsen did comedy. He danced, sang and played the saxophone. Bless his heart. He had to be push-ing ninety. What a great guy. Jane Wyman looked frail but great and Alice Faye died shortly thereafter. But, I thought she looked wonderful. She looked stronger and healthier than Jane Wyman. Luckily, Jane Wyman is still with us, which was very evident when Ronald Reagan passed away. It was a lovely show. Palm Springs High School has done lots of these kinds of shows with older entertainers who live here, famous people, and celebrities.

I opened Fantasy Springs Casino, an Indian Casino. They had the most beautiful showroom with these gorgeous scalloped silver drapes that looked like something out of New York and about 3 or $400,000 worth of lights and sound equipment. It was just a gorgeous room and I was there for six months. Ted Herman headed the band behind me and we had some great players like the Condoli brothers and Bob Corwin on piano. We packed the room and then found out they couldn't sell any liquor. They could sell liquor in the dining room but on the other side of the building their license wouldn't work. But, I did six months there and enjoyed every minute of it. I loved that room. I loved the sound, the lights. What a shame it's now a High-Rollers slot machine room. But, soft drinks and cappuccino only they couldn't make a go of it.

Milestones and Memories was a real pleasure. I was called by the Welk organization and told they wanted me to fly me back to Branson, Missouri to the Welk Resort and Theatre. They were filming a four hour special for KPBS. We worked all week, rehearsed for hours, and anyone who'd been in the band was there. Henry Questa, the clarinet player, Helen Ramsey, the girl whose place I took and many more were there. Barney Liddell, the trombone player from the band I was with was there too. He was the guy who drove the car with my mom and me while on the road, doing one-niters. I have to be honest with you. I had a crush on him. He was so handsome in those days. But I had to wear blinders because I wasn't even allowed to look at any of the guys in the band because Mr. Welk forbid it. The show was wonderful. It was a four hour show shot with five cameras in front of a live audience. The Lennon sisters were there. Arthur Duncan was there. Joanne Castle was there. Robby Burges, with all three dancers that he'd had over the years showed up. Jack Emmel, Anna Conti, who sang all the Latin songs, Guy and Rowna, and Norma Zimmer were there. I just love Norma. She had a different style. Lawrence Welk never really liked the high voices and yet George Cates, when he came on to do the conducting and arranging when Lawrence wasn't there, on the big band TV show, he needed the high voice because they were doing some Fred Waring style arrangements where they had a lot of singers and they didn't need to have a high voice. There were a lot of girls like myself, Helen O'Connell, Doris Day, the big band singers and we were considered illegitimate sopranos. We had a nice range. But we were not what were called Broadway type ingénues like Norma. What a lovely lady and adorable to work with. They had all four of the prior Champagne Ladies, but there were only two of us who did the TV show. That was Norma Zimmer and myself. Helen Ramsey and Lois Best were both prior to the TV show. But, on Milestones and Memories they had us all sitting in these high backed chairs holding bunches of roses. I felt like Queen for a Day. I thought it was a beautifully produced show and it's still on the air. People can still see it and order the show from KPBS.

The Fabulous Ladies of Song would probably be the show that I did at one of my favorite places, the McCallum Theatre at the Bob Hope Cultural Center in Palm Desert, California. We also did the Escondido Cultural Center, Orange Coast Performing and the Thousand Oaks Arts Centers and several more. It was with Florence Henderson, Betty Garrett, one of my favorite ladies in the world, Gloria Loren and myself. It was called the Fabulous Ladies of Song and it was also produced by Terry Hill and Associates. I have worked for him for many years. He does a lot of productions here. We ended the tour at the McCallum and were very well received. I thought the show was a hit. We packed every place we went. We sold our albums and signed autographs. Florence Henderson was a doll.

The last time that I saw Lawrence Welk, I had been invited to do the fifty year anniversary of television on KTLA; Bonnie, who was a producer of the show, had me taken in a limousine down to where the old Aragon ballroom used to be. The foundation is still there, off Lick Pier, but the Aragon had burnt down long before, years ago. I walked in the sand, did some memories on camera. Then afterwards, Bonnie asked me if I would like to go and see Lawrence. He was in his penthouse at the Champagne Towers in Santa Monica, right on the coast overlooking the ocean. The limo driver took me there and I went up in the elevator. Mrs. Welk came to the door. She had a little parakeet she loved sitting on her shoulder. She said, "Oh Roberta. It's so good to see you. I know Lawrence is going to love this." By this time Lawrence Welk was blind. He'd lost his eyesight and he was very frail.

I'd like to straighten this out. A lot of people said he had Alzheimer's. My personal opinion is I think he was just very depressed. He couldn't watch his shows anymore and he used to watch the reruns a lot. He loved to play golf and he couldn't do that anymore. So, he couldn't see he couldn't do the things he loved. Basically, it was old age and depression that was his demise.

Mrs. Welk walked me into the bedroom and Lawrence Welk was sitting on the side of the bed and I think his nurses name was Rose. She and Mrs. Welk both said, "Roberta Linn is here."

Lawrence starting crying as he said, "Oh, Ruperta. My little Champagne Lady. I love you so much."

I went over to him and he grabbed my hands and

kept kissing my hands while saying, "You were my favorite. You were my favorite." We talked for quite a while, reminiscing about the road days, the starting of the TV show, and so on. It was sad to see him like that because he was such a very vital man.

Shortly after that he passed away and we were all invited to the funeral. It was in the cemetery that Al Jolson was buried in; Rose Hills. The only way you could get into the private ceremony for the family and members of the band was to know the password: Dixieland. It was a beautiful service. Everyone talked about the days with Mr. Welk. At the end of the service we all marched behind the Dixieland band over to the gravesite and everybody sang "The Goodnight Song" which had come later in the history of the show as a closing song. I used to end the show by singing "I'll See You in My Dreams," which I'd sing and Lawrence would play the accordion. But, later on George Cates switched it and we all sang "The Goodnight Song," and that was the last time that I saw Lawrence Welk.

In conclusion, I have to say this.

When I came to the point of being tired of working on the road all the time, living out of a suitcase, in hotel rooms, I decided I had to make a change. And I worked just as hard in the little clubs as I did on the big stage in a big venue. Then the timeshare presentation came along and my friends would say, "What! You're doing timeshare. Isn't that below you?"

I thought at the time, Gee, what a thing to say. And then I realized, all of these people that were saying that to me were people that weren't working anymore. They couldn't get a job and suddenly here I was selling timeshares and singing when I wanted to. I could be more selective of the dates like when I did the Fabulous Ladies of Song and going and doing the Welk show and doing my Fantasy

In 2001, there was a gatering of all Welk's singers and musicians who were still alive and kicking at the Welk resort in Branson, Missouri

These days my big brother Bill and I live together at our home in Rancho Mirage, CA. It's nice to have someone I love to share my life with.

Betty Garrett, Florence Henderson, myself and Gloria Loring during the "Fabulous Ladies of Song" tour in 2002.

The Cathedral City Chamber of Commerce and the Senior Cneter worked together to host a fundraiser with me as the main act. I've always liked working with charities.

Springs stay. I did that, but in the meantime I still did my timeshare sales and I realized that even this late in my life, with all I'd been through, I could have a nice car, still have a nice home, have money in the bank and some security that some of the other friends of mine don't have because they time warped. They stay in the same time warp. They didn't progress with the time and were afraid to try something new.

It's OK to do nostalgia, but you gotta also know when you can insert a new number and create a new life for yourself.

I meet wonderful people doing my timeshares and I work with wonderful people. I work for a major company that has great prestige. But, I just want to insert this. This is where I am right now. Now I can sing when and where I want to. Not because I have to and I do love to sing and entertain.

ALMOST OLD AND ALMOST YOUNG

Almost old and almost young
It's enough to make you come unstrung
If you act a little silly
Your children say, "Mother Really…"
I guess that's just the way
They did things in your day

If you try to dance or dress in the latest style
They all smile and giggle for a little while
Oh, won't they let me be what I want to be
without making fun at what they see
For someday, they will be almost old and almost young
Just like me.

Roberta Linn

Roberta Linn

Credits

INTERNATIONAL TOURS
World Tours with Bob Hope
Oriental Tour – Bangkok, Singapore, Hong Kong, Okinawa, Tokyo, Jakarta, and the Philippines
Alaskan Tour with Clint Eastwood, Chill Wills and Maia Powers
Canadian Tour – "Sound of Glenn Miller" show, 10 major cities
Australian Tour – Sydney, Brisbane and Melbourne

TELEVISION
The Roberta Linn "Café Continental" coast-to-coast syndicated show – Winner of the TV Academy's Emmy Award
"Frosty Frolics" syndicated TV show, coast-to-coast
"The Lawrence Welk Show" (Original "Champagne Lady")
Johnny Carson's "Tonight Show"
The Mike Douglas Show
Sammy Davis Show
Regis Philbin Show
Joey Bishop Show

RECORDS
"Roberta"
"Roberta Linn sings the Hits"
"Help Me Make It Through the Night", 45 RPM Single –
was a "Pick Hit" with 124 Radio Stations
"Strangers When We Wake Up", 45 RPM Single
"Momma How'd I Din'" Country Pop
"Welfare Wire", Country Pop
"Roberta and All That Jazz"
"Champagne with Welk"

CONCERTS
Fabulous Ladies of Song – 2002 – with Florence Henderson, Betty Garrett and Gloria Loring
Escondido Symphony Orchestra
SeaWorld Amphitheatre with Super Band and the San Diego Symphony
Magic Mountain
Disneyland
Oriental Tour – 1980 – Japan, Singapore, Bangkok and Thailand
Canadian Tour – "Sound of Glenn Miller"
Branson, MO
Nashville, TN – Grand Ole Opry
Orange Coast College Performing Arts Series

MOVIES
"Get Yourself a College Girl"
"Idle Maker"

CAREER HIGHLIGHTS
SeaWorld's "Atlantis", San Diego – 5 Years – 1979to 1984
Hyatt Hotels
Holiday Inns – Memphis, Des Moines, Ventura, Torrance

(Main Rooms)
Sahara Hotels – Las Vegas and Lake Tahoe, NV – 5 yrs
Stardust Hotel – Las Vegas, NV – 136 weeks
Sheppard Drake Hotel – New York, NV
Caesar's palace – Las Vegas, NV
New Frontier Hotel – Las Vegas, NV
Riverside Hotel – Reno, NV
Mapes Hotel – Reno, NV
Harrah's – Lake Tahoe, NV
Beverly Hills Club – Kentucky
Sutmilleff's Dayton – Ohio
Century Plaza Hotel – Los Angeles, CA
Cal Neva – Lake Tahoe, NV
Fairmont Hotel – Tulsa, OK
Blue Room, Fairmont Hotel – New Orleans, LA
Plaza Hotel – New York, NY
Polumbo's – Philadelphia, PA
Sahara Inn – Phoenix, AZ
International Hotel – Winnipeg, Canada
Latin Quarter – Topkyo
Chase Hotel – St. Louis, MO
Eden Roc – Miami, FL
"Casino de Paris" Dunes Hotel – Las Vegas, NV
Americana Hotel – Puerto Rico
Empire Room, Palmer House – Chicago, IL
Hollywood Paladium – Hollywood, CA
Copacabana – New York, NY
Intercontinental Hotels – Aruba, Curacao
Loews Paradise Valley Resort – Scottsdale, AZ
Wyndham Hotel – Palm Springs, CA
Riverside Hotel – Laughlin, NV

Champagne Lady

CRUISES
SS Universe
SS Fairseas, Sitmar (Several Times)
Star Cruise
Hawaiian Cruise Lines
Princess Cruises

MISCELLANEOUS STARS, MOVIES AND EVENTS
"Anthony Adverse" with Olivia DeHaviland (Played her baby sister) – Warners
with Ronald Coleman (Played the crippled girl with Polio) – 20th Century
"Babes in Toyland" with Laurel and Hardy – Hal Roach Studios
"Curly Top" with Shirley Temple – 20th Century
"Little Colonel" with Shirley Temple – 20th Century

Conway Terril and Barbara Bedford at Grand Opening of "Senor Jim." Had star billing. Premier was at Million Dollar Theatre, downtown Los Angeles. Headlined a musical show; sang and danced and did a routine with Cab Calloway, who had the band in between movie showings.

"Our Gang Comedies"
Pat O'Brien
Randolph Scott
Ann Sheridan
Cary Grant
Sybil Jason
Jimmy Durante
Clark Gable
Bob Steele – "Gun Lords of Stirrup Basin"
Dick Powell
Pete Smith Shorts - "Life of Louis Pasteur" (Played girl attacked by rabid dog)

- "Last Days of Pompeii"
Al Jolson – Musical Scene, "Goin' to Heaven on a Mule"
Dorothy Lamour – "Jungle Princess" (Played her as a little girl) – Paramount
Martha Raye – "Ship Ahoy" Also played her as a little girl) – Paramount
Lawrence Welk – Musical Movie Shorts – Universal
"The Whistler" – While on staff at CBS
Did the lead in "Can Can" with Ricardo Montalban at the Circle Arts Theatre in the Round
Bit part in "IdolMaker"

COMMERCIALS
Max Factor (Print)
Gas Appliance Dealers of America (TV)
Chicken of the Sea (TV)
Chevrolet (TV)
Brill Cream (Did choreography for New York Jets)
Vitamin Commercials
Ford (Print)

Champagne Lady

Eric G. Meeks is a second generation rare book dealer and a former Barnes & Noble book seller. He's had several careers in his life: Chart House Cook, Jeep Salesman, Book Dealer, Marriott Executive, Real Estate Salesperson and Author. In 1976 he moved to Palm Springs, where he still lives with his wife Tracey and six of their seven children. The oldest one has already moved out and married.

To contact Eric directly: meekseric@hotmail.com

CPSIA information can be obtained at www.ICGtesting.com
Printed in the USA
BVOW012139130313

315520BV00008B/78/P

9 781478 171645